T0278137

WOMAN UP

WOMAN UP

Pitches, Pay and Periods: The Progress and Potential of Women's Football

Carrie Dunn

HERO, AN IMPRINT OF LEGEND TIMES GROUP LTD
51 Gower Street
London WC1E 6HJ
United Kingdom
www.hero-press.com

First published by Hero in 2023

© Carrie Dunn, 2023

The right of the author to be identified as the author of this work has
been asserted in accordance with the Copyright, Designs and Patents
Act 1988. British Library Cataloguing in Publication Data available.

Printed in Great Britain by Severn Print

ISBN: 978-1-91564-349-0

Prologue   3

Beginning   5
Preparation   33
Education   47
Clothes   69
Injuries   95
Bodies   125
Voice   157
Highs   183
Lows   207
Records   231

Acknowledgements   242

References   244

TO THE MAGNIFICENT WOMEN OF
ABERYSTWYTH TOWN WFC

THANK YOU FOR YOUR SPIRIT, YOUR FIGHT, YOUR
FRIENDSHIP — AND THE INSPIRATION

WOMAN UP

PROLOGUE

The past and present of women's football is much bigger than anyone imagines. With so few records existing of its earliest days, we are still piecing together its history; with so much growth happening so quickly on a global scale, we are struggling to keep up. This book is my way of telling the story of women's football since its inception and its development across the world, through an exploration of some of the challenges female footballers – of all standards, from the hobbyist to the top professional – have faced and continue to face in order to play the game they love. Every single woman who has ever pulled on a pair of boots has her own stories to tell; this is just the start, and there are so many tales I wanted to tell, plus many more tales that need to be told by those with lived experience and other perspectives. *Woman Up* is a series of snapshots, a plethora of pen portraits, giving an insight into a broad range of lives in football; it cannot be completely comprehensive (and by linguistic necessity includes many accounts from English-speaking nations, although I am incredibly grateful to those who have spoken to or emailed me in their second, third or even fourth language!), but there are some shared female experiences globally. Indeed, many of the amazing people to whom I have spoken have talked about several major hurdles they have faced, and faced down; though they may be included in one particular chapter, their stories may echo those of others found elsewhere in the book. Essentially, I hope here that I give a glimpse of the achievements of female footballers – and the complex, multiple obstacles they have had to overcome – ever since the birth of the game.

BEGINNING

Kicking a ball around with friends is one of the most straight-forward games for children to play. In its most basic form, it requires no expensive equipment, and not even a proper pitch, just a patch of grass or even tarmac, with teams of unorthodox, uneven numbers. In its more structured, codi-fied form, though, girls' and women's access to football has been massively limited.

Sometimes those restrictions have been societal. When women in Britain began to form football teams in the late nineteenth century with the intent to tour the country, some adopted pseudonyms – stage names for when they stepped on to a pitch – acknowledging that perhaps what they were doing would not be considered 'ladylike' and that this mat-tered to them. The captain of the British Ladies, the so-called 'Nettie Honeyball', was one of the players to do this, and her true identity is still a matter for much discussion. She was, however, careful to present herself as a respectable upper-middle-class woman, and was once quoted in the Maidenhead Advertiser as saying: "If I accepted all the girls from the masses that made application to join us, why, our list would have been filled long ago." This suggests that the women who did form the British Ladies were not "girls from the masses" but well-brought-up young ladies, or at least women who wanted to give that impression. They were also likely to be women with some degree of independence, without a husband, father or brother asserting his role as nominal head of the family to prevent her from playing, or perhaps an entirely supportive family encouraging her sporting pursuits, which would also have been less than usual at the time. There was certainly a prevailing belief – indeed, one that still exists in some quarters even now – that strenuous physical pursuits are not appropriate for the female body.

Sometimes those restrictions have, though, been entirely deliberate. In 1921, after women's exhibition matches continued to draw big crowds and big money, outside the auspices of their control, the FA began to worry. They permitted the celebrated factory team Dick, Kerr Ladies FC to play a South of England team at Bristol City with the condition that a full statement of accounts should be presented straight away. Then they told their member clubs that they needed prior permission before women could play a match on an affiliated pitch, regardless if it was for charity, and that the member club themselves would be responsible for the monies taken. This was followed by a notorious declaration in December:

> Complaints having been made as to football being played by women, Council feel impelled to express their strong opinion that the game is quite unsuitable for females and should not be encouraged.
>
> Complaints have also been made as to the conditions under which some of the matches have been arranged and played, and the appropriation of receipts to other than

charitable objects. The Council are further of the opinion that an excessive proportion of the receipts are absorbed in expenses and an inadequate percentage devoted to charitable objects.

For these reasons the Council requests the Clubs belonging to the Association refuse the use of their grounds for such matches.

This declaration made it extremely difficult for women to play football; male players and coaches were threatened with sanctions should they assist any female footballers or their teams. Similar attitudes were evident elsewhere; the Federation Française de Football (FFF) was founded in France in 1919, and although they did not ban women's football outright, they did not accept women's teams as members. Nevertheless, female players continued, seeking out scrubland, rugby pitches and public parks, even though they were not acknowledged by their country's governing bodies. This happened across the world, with those institutions less than interested in supporting the women's game and choosing instead to ignore it, until that course of action became impossible. Independent bodies – such as the Women's FA running a domestic competition in England from 1969, the German Ladies' Football Association doing similar in West Germany, and the Federation of Independent European Female Football (FIEFF) operating across the continent of Europe – were proving that there was a demand for women's football, with a possible commercial benefit. Unofficial European Championships and World Cups were organised and attracted thousands of fans, yet those who participated paid a high price; Harry Batt, who took a team from Britain to Mexico in 1971, received a life ban from the game on his return, with his players receiving shorter sanctions. Inevitably, the official authorities wanted to bring it under their domain and their control. UEFA and FIFA began to recognise and integrate the women's game from 1971 onwards, encouraging national associations to take responsibility for women's football, but it has been a slow and in many instances reluctant progress. When official international tournaments were organised, the powers-that-be were still loath to bestow their established brand names on women's competitions; in 1984, the first European Championship was called the European Competition for Women's Football, while in 1991 the first World Cup was called, astoundingly, the First FIFA World Championship for Women's Football for the M&Ms Cup.

The FA took their time considering how best to organise a domestic league for women, assessing how other countries had succeeded or struggled with their own competitions, and subsequently delaying the launch of the semi-professional Women's Super League until the summer of 2011. Within a decade, the WSL was fully professional, with promotion and relegation to a semi-professional second tier. By the end of 2022, England had won only their second major senior trophy ever as Sarina Wiegman's Lionesses lifted the European Championship.

This was a significant achievement for women's football, but girls' football has continued to face problems. Although there has been a growing network of women's clubs, girls in

England have struggled to find teams to represent, with many either giving up or playing for a boys' team; former Arsenal and England winger Rachel Yankey cut her hair short and called herself 'Rae' as a child to avoid being identified as a girl.

Perhaps the most famous example of a girl who fought hard for the right to play football was Theresa Bennett, who was twelve when her coach rang her to tell her she was not allowed to play football for their team that season. If she did, he said, the whole team would be banned from competition. This was because she was a girl, and the rest of the players in the league were boys.

In June 1979, Bennett was adjudged to be a victim of unlawful sex discrimination by the Football Association and the Nottinghamshire FA, who stopped her from playing with the Muskham United under-12 boys' team. The rule at the time was that mixed football was not permitted, and Bennett sought help from the Equal Opportunities Commission, with the full support of her parents and a solicitor who was happy to work pro bono. She was awarded £200 in damages by deputy circuit judge Michael Harris at Newark County Court after being prevented from playing the previous season, along with £50 for the injury to her feelings; it was accepted at that hearing that before puberty there were no real physical differences between boys and girls.

Naturally, the FA appealed. The case ended up in the High Court, but Bennett and her parents were only told about it at 5.30am on the morning of the hearing. Neither her mother nor her father could drive, and by the time they had got the train to London, the ruling had been made in the FA's favour, and Bennett had not had chance to say anything. The nearest women's team to Bennett was in Nottingham, twenty-two miles away, and as she was unable to travel there until she could drive herself, she did not play football again until she was seventeen.

The Bennett case was famous; inspirational for many, perhaps, but also indicative of the obstacles that remained for girls wanting to play football, even though the FA had ostensibly rubber-stamped it. Even in the twenty-first century, football has still been seen as a boys' sport, with girls' access restricted. According to the FA's data from 2021, football was – perhaps unsurprisingly – the most popular sport for children in England, but only one third of girls aged between five and eighteen were able to play every week. More than that, 91 per cent of girls who were not able to play football in their school PE lessons would have liked to be able to – but only 67 per cent of all schools (41 per cent of secondary schools) offered football equally to girls in PE lessons, with 46 per cent of schools providing the same extracurricular opportunities as boys.

These are the fundamental statistics that underpin the FA's Let Girls Play campaign, which launched in October 2021 and picked up masses of momentum following the Lionesses' win at the 2022 European Championships. The England squad's open letter to then-prime ministerial candidates Liz Truss and Rishi Sunak grabbed the headlines, with many onlookers shocked about the limited resources that were still available for girls to play what had long been considered the national sport.

"The reality is we are inspiring young girls to play football, only for many to end up going to school and not being able to play," the footballers wrote. "This is something that we all experienced growing up. We were often stopped from playing. So we made our own teams, we travelled across the country and despite the odds, we just kept playing football. Women's football has come a long way. But it still has a long way to go."

The FA and their corporate partners offered a variety of grassroots programmes specifically for girls: the Wildcats, a non-competitive programme for girls aged between five and eleven, and Squad Girls, a progression for girls aged between twelve and fourteen. On International Women's Day 2023, the FA and the government announced that girls would have equal access to football in schools as part of an all-sport commitment.

"By making football more accessible to millions of girls across the nation, we have opened a crucial door for the growth of women's football and women's sport as a whole," said Lotte Wubben-Moy, one of the Lionesses who had spear-headed the campaign for more girls to play football. "I am proud to be part of something that will live on for generations to come. This is just the beginning."

The American Youth Soccer Organization is the oldest national youth soccer programme in the United States. Founded in 1964 in California, the non-profit began with just nine teams and a few volunteers who wanted to bring young people into football – or 'soccer', as it tends to be called in the USA. Although the sport had been played there for a century previously, it was not one of the most popular sports there, superseded by baseball and American football. Despite men having their own nationwide competition, it was fraught with organisational and governance difficulties as well as finance issues, and had dropped out of the public eye by the time AYSO launched.

The launch of AYSO was followed by the launch of the new professional North American Soccer League for men; thirty years later, in 1995, an amateur league for women, the W-League, began. Soccer was by this time a sport that was more popular for girls and women than for boys and men, in no small part to the financial investment that followed the introduction of Title IX, to assure equal access to sport for women and men within academic institutions. The achievements of the US women's national team (USWNT) solidified its attraction for the following generations; a Women's World Cup win in 1991, then an Olympic gold medal in 1996 also thrust celebrity on its star players, such as Mia Hamm, who was so recognisable that she even got mentioned in an episode of the hit sitcom *Friends*.

AYSO's mission is for everyone to be able to play football; every player on a team must play at least 50 per cent of every game, and every year new teams are created with the intention of making them as evenly balanced as possible, ensuring competitive matches that are also productive learning experiences for everyone. As with most football organisations, AYSO is reliant on volunteers to run and coach teams as well as referee matches.

Scott Snyder was a player himself before moving into coaching and strategy, and was later appointed as AYSO's senior director of sport development.

"It comes down to creating an environment that is conducive for a child to play soccer, and that's how I view it, even though some people see it a little bit more complicated than that," he explained. "At the end of the day, anything I put down in words, and then train someone on, will equate to an environment on a local field somewhere, [where a] child will get into the parents' car and turn to Mom or Dad and say, 'Hey, that was cool, and I can't wait to go back' or 'I don't want to go back.'"

One of his challenges was ensuring that volunteers got the training they needed to be able to coach teams, particularly parents – often mothers – who were coming forward and offering to step up so that their daughters had a place to play. Since the Covid-19 pandemic, a virtual option had been embedded in the training offering, but a balance needed to be struck to ensure that volunteers also had experience of coaching on a pitch with players.

"Our balance becomes what is appropriate for online content, review and participation, and then how do we get into the field to do some field work or watch a demonstration? Can you watch it on a video? You can. Did they get that same experience? No. So where's the trade-off?" he said.

"It's particularly important for volunteer parent coaches because their currency is their time. If I'm a professional coach, then I'll go wherever I need to go, it will be paid for by my club – and great. But if I've got two full-time jobs, and my kids to keep an eye on, can we be realistic? That's what it's about: being respectful and being realistic, too, and providing people with enough information they feel confident enough to stay involved, because if they feel out of their depth or uncomfortable, maybe they won't stay involved."

AYSO, like many other volunteer-led organisations across the country, was a member of the game's governing body, US Soccer. The twenty-first century had seen the establishment of thriving professional leagues for men and women, meaning that there was now a pathway for both boys and girls to progress to elite competition should they wish. As a former elite player himself, Snyder knew that the very best players would always get their opportunities to shine.

"Talent gets you through that," he said. "You're going to get picked, you're going to get through it. No top elite athlete goes unfound."

He did have a concern for the majority of players, though – those not on the so-called 'performance pathway' to the very top, but those playing 'recreational soccer'. Snyder felt that 'rec soccer' had been typically looked down upon because it was not about elite achievement, but pointed out that the pandemic had shown just how important it was to offer sport as a leisure and social pursuit.

"Everything was taken away [during the pandemic]. So were kids really training every day on their own and doing all the skills? No. They just wanted to socialise and play with their buddies. So I think there's a new recognition and a respect for those children that just want to participate in a social sporting environment," he said, adding that the elite performance pathway in many places had been monetised, with more and more players being encouraged into it because it brought in revenue, but then ultimately dropping out of the sport because of the expense and the amount of time it required.

"If you just want to play and have fun and socialise with your buddy, great, just stay in the game. We're losing players… we're not growing at the rate we should be considering the initial population playing."

Snyder spoke from personal experience. His daughter had stopped playing soccer during the pandemic, leaving the 'performance pathway' along with many of her team-mates. Like many other people, the girls had considered the best use of their free time, and analysed what they enjoyed most about football, and had ultimately decided that playing at a high level of competition was not what attracted them.

"The socialisation part prior to training – or during – is really important, but what do coaches do? 'Stop talking, come on, let's focus, we should be practising.' This is some of the nuances of coaching girls versus boys, mostly. That's an important element regardless of the pathway. Socially, that's an important element that girls have a lot more than boys – boys have it as well, but to a lesser extent. If you substitute that or remove that opportunity [to socialise], it's a different dynamic."

AYSO's mission statement was to provide world-class soccer coaching that enriched children's lives, and Snyder's argument was that such a target could not be achieved if the focus was solely on improving a player. Instead, what was necessary was to find ways to use football coaching to deliver life lessons, such as good sportsmanship or citizenship.

"It'll be a much richer environment, and genuinely, I feel, a better value for money for parents that pay money to participate, which is a factor here," he added. Finance in youth sport was a big consideration, especially in the US, where a lot of travel could be required even from recreational teams. Again, Snyder was aware how problematic and off-putting this could be for young people and their families based on his own experience with his daughter.

"It adds up significantly," he said, highlighting that often a parent would travel with their child, meaning that costs were further exacerbated. "There's hotels, food, there's petrol, and it adds up."

Snyder was adamant that there was nothing recreational about playing a competitive sport; it was just a question of prioritising different elements of the game. He thought that valuing the social aspect of playing sport was a healthier and more realistic attitude, particularly for young people. AYSO had begun to develop ways to embed social and emotional learning into its coaching offering, enabling coaches to help their players develop as well-rounded individuals.

"As a coach I'm looking at the Xs and Os [losses and wins] but I'm also looking at leadership, I'm looking at self-awareness. My viewpoint is completely broadened by that thought. Does it take away from the Xs and Os? Not really, it just adds to it, but it's an important element. We're getting some great success and interest in that idea of being a lot more holistic in our contribution than just Xs and Os and I think in particular for female athletes, there's more opportunity there. There's as much for boys and girls, [but] the girls are a lot more open to it, because you can connect there, there's a different type of rapport you can develop."

"You do team sports – why don't you set up a session?"

Christina Philippou's journey into football coaching in England was unorthodox. After reading a polemic about women's sport with her book club, they suggested that she should run a group for beginner female footballers. Four years on, there were seventy women signed up, with between ten and twenty turning up to have a kickaround every week. She started coaching children, however, in a much more usual way, after having her children. Unable to take part in her habitual exercise routines after less-than-straightforward births, she began volunteering with Onslow FC. Volunteer coaches are often difficult to come by, particularly with the younger age groups; while clubs depend on parents coming forward, many do not want to give up their time until they are sure that their own children will be interested in attending week in, week out. Philippou had three children – two boys and a girl – and led the mixed-sex under-six squad for five years.

"I'm not the world's most patient person, so it's been very good for my development to basically run nursery classes for five years!" she laughed. "What I tried to do from the start was encourage girls to come in, make it very open – this is mixed, and I made it very clear that we would take literally anybody."

The under-sixes are small, and often quite scared of being in a new environment, seeking comfort from their parents on the sidelines.

"It doesn't matter," she said. "So long as they enjoy themselves, I don't care if they come off and then go to their parents for a bit and then come back on. Just let them do their own thing, it's perfectly fine, it's perfectly normal."

One pattern that she did see emerging was rather more frustrating. If a little girl was not sure about football after one session, her parents would likely not bring her back; if a little boy was not so keen, he would still attend week after week.

"'Oh yeah, they're not interested, they're more into their dance' – do you realise they can do both, they can enjoy dancing and football? Groundbreaking! That was quite a hard slog," she admitted. Nonetheless, some girls stayed on; Philippou estimated that around a fifth of the players across the age groups were girls, and Onslow FC's coaches worked hard to keep them on, ensuring that they had friends and solidarity in their teams and training squads regardless of how good they were as players.

"We've been very conscious of making sure that when we break them up into teams to play leagues that we keep a critical mass of girls," she explained. "When we did the streaming, we went, 'Right, what's the ratio of boys to girls in the club? We're going to do that ratio of girls in the top team.' It's not like, 'OK, here's nine boys and one girl in the top [team] just because it's on ability'; we've gone, 'There should be three girls and seven boys' or whatever the ratio was and that's what we're going to do. That's meant that quite a lot of them have continued.

"We tried to keep the friends together as well. We asked the parents which girls are their friends from school, so we can just put them together, even [when] ability-wise it didn't quite match up. It was more about making sure they have a group because a lot of what I've seen in my sons' years, there were a couple of girls who we've got in and then they dropped off. I've seen where there's one or two in a team it's much harder to sustain keeping them on whereas when you've got a group of them [it's easier], and then when we do training we make sure we train all of [the players] together, so even if they're not with their friends on their teams, because the skill level is so diverse then at least at training they get to play with their friends, so it's very much about keeping that community."

The emphasis was on having fun. Results were unimportant ("Obviously we would quite like you to win, but we don't care if you're losing – are you enjoying yourself? Did you improve? Did you score? Did you block something?") and that attitude had helped to retain girls in a mixed set-up. Philippou had found that some girls did not want to move to an all-girls environment and did not want to join a girls' club; some did, which was the best thing for them, but for others, the mixed set-up was more fun; and for still others, they wanted to play in both types of team.

"As long as they're staying in the game, I'm not really fussed," said Philippou. She found that some girls started playing football midway through primary school, by which time they were already behind the boys who had been signed up to a team at a much earlier age, so sometimes an all-girls environment was much more supportive and fun.

"They develop so quickly at that age as well, it's just amazing. Some of the kids that we had that just couldn't kick a ball last year are now doing phenomenal things on the pitch and a lot of it's about confidence, especially with girls that are interested in football and come into it at a later age – it tends to be because they're fairly sporty anyway and it's not as if the base skill isn't there, it's just that this is football as opposed to this is some other sport they have been playing."

Though Onslow FC had currently paused its intake due to a lack of coaches, Philippou knew that the success of England's Lionesses and their increased media profile had boosted the number of girls playing at the local girls-only club.

"It shows how important it is to have female role models that are shown on telly, that are in the news, as opposed to 'Here's the afterthought.'"

She also noticed that with mixed teams, even at such a young age, it was less likely they would hear sexist comments on the sidelines.

"I grew up with brothers and I grew up being one of the only girls [playing mixed sport], but I feel it's a really good way of people just seeing [women playing football] as the norm. I love that my kids go, 'Oh, it's Man City-Arsenal on the telly!' and I say, 'Really? I didn't know they were playing! Oh, it's the women,' and we see that attitude across a lot of our teams, which is quite nice, but I think it takes a lot of hard work. It's been a lot harder to try and encourage girls to come in, and parents of girls to bring them. It's basically selling the mixed message repeatedly to try and get them, because otherwise people just assume it's for boys. [We] say we are open to anyone, but it's not necessarily clear that 'anyone' means girls as well sometimes, I think those attitudes are unfortunately still there, particularly with the parents, so I think it's about breaking that down."

Girls-only and women-only teams were far tougher to find in the UK than one for only males or those with a mixed junior section. It meant that those wishing to play in a female-only environment often had to travel a significant distance to reach a club with the ethos they wanted. As with most grassroots clubs, those only for female players rarely had paid staff to keep things running; they needed to rely on the commitment of volunteers.

Sometimes they were reliant on those already in football who had been inspired by women's stories and their dedication to the game despite all the obstacles. Take, for instance, Harry Cuthbert, who had never watched women's football before, let alone girls' football back in 2018, three years after the Lionesses had won the bronze medal at the Women's World Cup; that achievement had not captured his attention as he concentrated his efforts on coaching boys. Then his brother suggested he join him at AFC Leyton, a grassroots independent club for female players based in East London, and invited him down to a session.

"It was so good. I absolutely loved it, and I've been here ever since," he explained. He took on the role of club chairman in

2022, feeling it was a great opportunity to help progress an aspect of the sport he had come to love. He had been able to make direct comparisons between his experience of coaching a team of boys and coaching a team of girls, and had noticed how difficult it was for AFC Leyton to get hold of what he described as "safe" pitch space – where small girls would not be scared or intimidated by a squad of grown men waiting for their turn on the community Astroturf.

The success of the Lionesses had led to lots of girls wanting to join AFC Leyton's sessions, but the club was not able to accommodate them as they were unable to afford the extra pitch time. As Cuthbert pointed out, girls' teams linked to men's clubs who owned their own stadium had much more chance of being able to access some space. He admitted that AFC Leyton had considered a formal collaboration with a men's club for that exact reason.

"We just thought, 'No,'" he said, "because what makes us unique and what makes us special is that we don't have that. We try and fight and break down the barriers that we are trying to face.

"It is girls only. Lots of people love that. Lots of girls that are coming in have been with boys' teams in the past or been with mixed teams, and they have just said to their parents, 'I want to play in a girls' team', and obviously doing that the way we do it means they get that safe space, they get that nice environment that they're looking for."

AFC Leyton offered a variety of sessions for all age groups. Some were pay-as-you-play drop-in squads; others played regularly in competitive leagues. One of the initiatives Cuthbert was proudest of was the "Just Play" session that welcomed absolute beginners.

"They email, and say, 'Look, I've never played before, I want to come in,'" he said. "They just always go, 'Am I going to be bad? Am I going to be rubbish?' For me, it's the best bit when actually I go, 'Don't stress. Don't worry. You've got twenty other ladies in the same position. Just come in. Enjoy it.'

"At the end of the session, they're red-faced, they're sweating, they're absolutely blowing, they're tired, but they've loved it. Providing that one hour a week to get rid of work or family or stress issues, whatever it is, they really do appreciate it, and it makes us, yeah, it makes us feel really good about ourselves.

"I'm a man, I've grown up around football, it's always been around, it's always been accessible in PE in school all the way through and you can just walk a hundred yards up the road and you'll probably find a boys' club, but in the girls and for the ladies it's completely different. We're super happy that we can do that. We would never stop doing that. In the next fifteen years when it continues to grow there will still be new people that go, 'You know what? I want to get involved,' and we'll continue to provide that."

Other female-only clubs were founded and run in the most traditional of styles – parents taking on the coaching and management roles after realising that their daughters had nowhere to play locally.

Gwyn Roberts's daughter gave up her regular swimming sessions, and was told by her parents that if she was not going to swim, then she had to find another physical activity to do. She picked up a leaflet at school for a football taster day and said she would like to try it out, and began going to sessions after school and at the weekend in a local leisure centre in Caerphilly, Wales. The one thing she did not love about it was the fact that she was one of only a handful of girls amidst a sea of boys, and there were no girls-only teams in the immediate local area that worked with her existing school and extra-curricular schedule. A women's club in Caerphilly was interested in setting up a junior section, so Roberts and another father of a football-playing daughter took that task on, before becoming an independent club, Caerphilly Dragons, a few years later as the numbers boomed.

The intake continued to grow, with a senior women's team the latest addition, meaning that the under-16s had somewhere to move on to after ageing out of the junior section. The women's side was primarily made up of mothers of girls already playing at the club.

"We thought, 'We've got 250 girls playing at various age groups – there must be one or two mums out there that would be interested in playing, whether new or they used to play before,' so we set it up, put a message out to all the parents, we had quite a lot of interest straight away."

Parents also remained a key part of the coaching set-up. With every age group, Roberts and his colleagues would keep an eye out for any parents who seemed like they might be interested in helping out in a more formal role, approaching them and offering to support them through coaching courses should they wish to become more involved.

"Our motto is fun, friendship, fair play," he said, "and we try and make sure we've got that ethos throughout the club.

So that attracts people to us. It's predominantly fathers at the moment as well, which is good that we've got the people to be able to coach, but we certainly want more mums and more women to be able to feel confident to be able to do that."

Roberts was also keen to encourage some of the older girls to try out leadership roles with the younger age groups, giving them role models to emulate. The only real roadblock was access to pitch space, as they needed more and more as the number of girls wanting to join the club rose. He was hoping that at some point they would be able to sign a long-term lease on an external facility, giving them a solid home base and the opportunity to apply for funding to improve and expand the space in the future.

"If somebody had told me three, four years ago I [would be] running what I think is the largest girls-only football team in Wales, I'd never have believed them," he admitted.

"I have always wanted to own my own club."

Nicole Allison had always had a dream. As a former player in England herself, primarily for Wolverhampton Wanderers, and then as the general manager of Tottenham Hotspur Women, supporting them as they achieved promotion into the FA Women's Super League, she developed some strong ideas about how women's football clubs should be run. During the Covid-19 pandemic, she – like many others – took the opportunity to consider the direction of her life and career, and kept coming back to that long-held ambition.

"I wanted to own my own club, actually make my own decisions and start things from almost the bottom right the way through to the top, because I knew at Tottenham I could make certain changes, but ultimately it's a global brand that have got their ways of working. Even though they say women's football is a priority on their agenda – and it's better than it ever has been there – but the men's team are always going to be number one. So I wanted to start something where women's and girls' [football] was always going to be number one."

Together with her wife Gill, Allison developed plans to move back to her home city of Worcester. Then she had a chance conversation with a Tottenham fan she had met during her time at the club and enjoyed being able to give back to the sport he loved, who suggested that if she did run her own football club, he would invest in it. Allison approached Worcester City and asked what the situation was with their women's team – or 'ladies' team', as it was called then. They entered discussions to hand it over to Allison and her investor as co-owners, who set up their own limited company enabling the women's team to operate as a separate entity.

"I felt like there was such a huge opportunity to have a professional football club in Worcester," said Allison. "Football isn't really on the agenda in Worcester whatsoever. It's obviously more of a rugby city and then cricket in the summer, but it's just crying out for something in football that people can really get behind. When I really started looking into the research of where women's and girls' football was in Worcestershire, whether it [had] moved on from when I was a player growing up [here], nothing had changed.

"When I was growing up twenty-five years ago here, I would not have been able to play at the level that I did if it wasn't for my dad driving back and forth to Wolverhampton three times a week. As you get older, you realise how lucky and privileged you are that you had a parent that could do that. I know so many people that have grown up and played in this area that have had to move away from Worcester to go and play: Birmingham, Wolves, Villa, even Leicester, Derby, some of them now.

"I was like, 'No, we want to create the talent here – and even bring and keep the talent to Worcester.' It's got a brilliant university that focuses on sport as well, which is growing. The city itself has got 100,000 people and is a really, really nice city to live in; a lot of people now are young professionals and families that are working in Birmingham, but living in Worcester. It's well connected: three train stations, just off the M5. I was like, 'This has got everything in the right place to have a really successful women's football team.'"

Fresh ideas are not always met receptively. Coaches and volunteers did not like the new set-up when it was announced in February 2021 and stood down immediately, and all Allison was left with, as lower-league women's football edged out of pandemic-induced restrictions, was around fifty players across three squads: the under-18s, the development team (or the reserves) and the first team. 2021/22 was the new regime's first full season in charge, and by 2022/23 they had a coaching team in post, plus a solid first-team squad that had benefited from a strong recruitment network. Everyone involved was still a volunteer, and Allison had made her policy clear: nobody would receive payment until the club was promoted into the National League (tier four), one tier above their current status in the West Midlands Regional Women's Football League.

Although she was pleased with how players and staff had bought into the values and culture she had set out for Worcester City Women, Allison acknowledged that there were still "endless curveballs" that came with running a football club. Local businesses did not realise that the women's team were not reliant on or run by the men's club: "They think that I'm just someone that's a volunteer coming to lead the women's stuff because I'm a woman."

Allison took inspiration from what she was seeing in the USA with Angel City FC – a football club with only a women's team, not a franchise that had both men and women competing in their leagues at the top level. She hoped that if they achieved promotion into the National League, they would benefit from a slightly more professional set-up, pointing to problems they had already faced, from late postponement of matches to lack of officials to take charge of games. She also hoped she would be dealing with league and club administrators with rather more progressive outlooks; she had previously faced backlash from some for introducing ticket prices for the women's matches.

"I wanted to put a value on watching the game," she explained. "We were playing at the same place the men's [team] were playing on a Saturday. We play on a Sunday. You wouldn't expect to walk up and watch for free on a Saturday to watch the men's [team] even though they're at the really low end of the men's football [the Midland League, tier nine]. I got told that I was a disgrace and starting a slippery slope for women's football because I was putting a ticket price on."

Allison appreciated that some teams in their league were not as fortunate as Worcester City Women. Her club played at Claines Lane, the base of the Worcestershire FA, and had access to a stand with seats, plus a set of volunteers that helped to steward car parking as well as show fans into the ground. Other teams were playing on pitches in playing fields, and charging for entry was not an option for them. However, even at tier five, competing cost money.

"We have to pay referees, we have to pay for the facility," she said. "Then you've got floodlights – with the cost of energy, that's gone up. If you're not going to charge for tickets, how do they expect that money to come back?"

Allison wanted to see more collaboration between clubs, as had been the case when she was working at Tottenham and liaised with all the other general managers in the league, but feared that short-term planning and short-sighted attitudes from some quarters would limit such collegial approaches. Of course, there was the added issue that many involved with women's teams were part of a parent club, and treated their associated men's club as a greater priority – just what Allison was avoiding with the independence of Worcester City Women.

"At Tottenham, we all got together as general managers – there was a sense of collective, and [the belief that] we're doing this to better the game," she said. "Certain decisions might not have suited a particular club, but they saw the bigger picture and they recognised that we needed that.

"At this level, there's no real collective agreement on anything, and that's something that I would love to try and change if I could. Having more women involved definitely helps, but it is, at this level, so male-dominated."

There was a huge team of matchday volunteers, from a former player who helped Allison with operations and logistics, to a university student who dealt with the social media channels.

"I don't believe in financial motivation being a long-term strategy for anything, so for me, it's about 'what value does this football club give back to these people?' If you're a volunteer, you must love volunteering because you give back to something. But I recognised that we were all a little bit chaotic in that, great, we had the volunteers but what were we really giving back to them, and how can I prove what we were giving back to them? So we did a focus group with them about what do they want back [from us] and they've never really been asked that question before!"

Some were part of volunteer organisations who needed their hours signed off to prove their dedication to the community; younger ones needed certification for their Duke of Edinburgh awards. Just by creating more of a process around recognising people's hours of volunteering, more volunteers were attracted to the club because they saw that it was an arrangement of mutual benefit.

"They feel very valued," said Allison, who was immensely grateful for all the help she got, particularly on a busy matchday "when I'm running round like a headless chicken half the time." She also had one particular member of the team who she had enlisted from a little closer to home.

"My wife does all the food on a matchday. There's a little hatch to sell teas, coffees, and chocolate bars. We didn't want it to be like the men's [games with] burgers and pies, we wanted it to be totally different. So what is fairly easy to do, but a bit different? We went with nachos, and it has just grown massively now. People are coming in, watching the football, enjoying their nachos, and it's become part of the whole fan experience: you don't get Worcester City Women without nachos and you don't get nachos without Worcester City Women."

Talent identification was something Allison was keen to promote. She knew from her own experience that it could be tough to find a club that was both local enough for someone working or studying full-time but also playing at a high enough level to provide a good standard of football. She had volunteers now dealing with any email enquiries from potential players who got in touch.

"We aren't a community club where we just accept anybody, we are about high performance," she said. "We do try and signpost people to other clubs if they're not right for us, because we are all people that want to try and help women play football."

Allison was hopeful that in the future Worcester City Women would be able to establish an academy system for elite youth players so that the best female players in the area would not have to travel into Birmingham or Wolverhampton for coaching or competition.

"There are some great grassroots clubs around the area and I don't want to come in and be another one of those," she said. "We want to have a club in the city where the top players, the best under-14s, the best under-15s can go and train and have the best training facilities, the best coaches."

Worcester City Women were in the earliest stages of what Allison expected would be a journey towards the top of the women's game. She knew that running a women's team independently of a well-off men's club would be difficult, particularly if the intent was to move towards semi-professionalisation, with payment on offer for players and staff. However, she did not regret leaving the elite of the women's game in order to pursue her dream.

"You feel like you are constantly fighting that battle every day to prove your worth, to just get space at the training ground," she reflected on her time working in the highest leagues. "Just do this, do that, and I was like, 'No. My energy is better spent somewhere else where actually I can grow something over the next twenty, thirty years and that's the legacy I'm going to leave."

She added: "I can make any decision I want, which is great. There are people that want to help, want to work with me, that bring different skill sets that I don't have, and different experiences that I don't have.

"I don't have to think about what the men's team do. We've got an opportunity where as a city and as a women's football club, we are going to be higher and bigger and better."

PREPARATION

Wendy Owen did not know a thing about defending until she was called up to the first-ever official England training camp in 1972. That was despite having played centre-half for her entire footballing career thus far. With little, if any, specialised training for positions, and with most coaches in the women's game keen volunteers rather than qualified professionals, it was perhaps not surprising that Owen writes in her footballing memoir *Kicking Against Tradition* that her eighteen-year-old eyes were entirely opened when she met Eric Worthington, the man given the task of coaching the first official England side. A former player himself, he was one of the FA's elite coaches and a lecturer at Loughborough College (now Loughborough University). He introduced Owen to the idea of defending with patience, holding off on a challenge rather than diving in, the concept of moving the attacking player wider.

Before England's first-ever match, against Scotland in Greenock, the squad had an entire day of training together, at the famous Bisham Abbey. It was Worthington's only chance to create a team with spirit and with a strong game plan, drilling them in set pieces; improving their fitness at that point would have been impossible. In the first years of the England team's official existence, an individual's fitness was her own responsibility. The coach might send out an information sheet summarising everything that had been covered in a camp. John Adams, who took over from Worthington, sent a letter to the squad ahead of his first international camp in 1973, telling them that the first day in training would be centred around shuttle runs, with any player unable to complete the required number jettisoned from the starting eleven. Desperate to make that team, Owen pushed herself through a fitness regime that involved jogging to build stamina, and sprint circuits to build speed.

Sue Lopez, another player from the start of the Lionesses' official history, wrote in her own book *Women on the Ball* of the lack of knowledge about diet, nutrition and fitness in those early years. She also drew a stark contrast with teams from other countries, such as Sweden and Italy, who had stolen a march on England and already in the early 1970s had players of greater skill and athleticism thanks to greater investment and better training facilities. Two decades later, when Lopez took on the leadership role of the Women's FA international officer, some elements had improved. Martin Reagan, who coached England from 1979 to 1990, had brought in important changes to help players with their fitness, having realised that the challenges of international women's football were huge; the amateur players had limited time to prepare for matches, could not focus entirely on their game because of their full-time jobs, and at the point where he took over they did not have the infrastructure to improve their fitness ahead of international matches. With a £6,000 grant from the Sports Council – who provided financial support for amateur sport

– England players were able to take six fitness tests every year, and over the course of a two-year period each received an individualised programme, meaning that even without regular training camps she could still follow expert advice and improve her physical condition.

Nevertheless, Lopez noted that some matters still had not improved; it was next to impossible to get hold of adequate training kits for the England squad. In the 1970s, players had trained in their own tracksuits; in 1991, they had drill suits provided, but this was still not ideal. Very few were in sizes to fit the players, with Lopez reporting that they were either much too big or much too small. Even with the England training regime so much improved under Reagan's tenure, the simple physical fact of the body of the female footballer still caused a crisis for the authorities.

Picking up dog faeces from a park is not the best preparation for the final of a major tournament, but that was what Anette Borjesson and her Sweden team found themselves doing in 1984. They were in the final of the first-ever European Championship for women – or as it was officially known, the European Competition for Women's Football. It was not one big tournament across the space of a few weeks; this was the pre-professional era, so players were taking time off work to be able to fit in these international fixtures. Sweden made it to the final to face England in a tie that would be contested across two legs, home and away, with the Swedes hosting the first match, and the English the second two weeks later, at Luton's Kenilworth Road. Captain Borjesson may have expected some training facilities to be laid on for them, but she was disappointed. Instead, they were offered the use of a park pitch, but it had to be cleared of the mess left by local dog walkers first, and it was the players who had to do it.

The weather in Bedfordshire did not help either their training or the match: a deluge of rain turned the pitch into a bog, hardly conducive to good football, but there was no reserve date possible. The match had to be played there and then, and Borjesson captained her side to a win after a penalty shoot-out. She had been skipper since her second game in the national team, and in retrospect she attributed it to the leadership skills she had developed while playing another sport at the highest level – badminton. Within two years of taking it up as a child, she was in the junior national team; in 1973 she won the senior championships despite still being a junior by age.

"It just rolled on," she said. "That year also I got to go to Indonesia for one month in our training camp in [19]73. That's huge. Nobody took those trips at that time. Today it's like nothing, but at that time I didn't have one friend that had been outside Europe or even maybe outside Sweden. Badminton was very important to me because of the travelling and exciting things I got to do."

It also helped her with her fitness and strength during the football season. Badminton training started in August with tournaments from October, finishing in around April. Then pre-season for football began, ending in October.

"For me, I could do the [badminton] pre-season training at

the same time I was playing soccer, it was good for me. I can easily say I had the best physical skills in my team."

Borjesson's club team-mates at Jitex agreed, and decided to imitate her training in order to improve their own physical capacities. Badminton requires strong legs, so Borjesson would do interval runs, sometimes up and down hills. Her team-mates did not need to join in her more badminton-specific training, such as "shadow badminton", playing the shots without an opponent, but it improved Borjesson's reflexes and gave her more explosive power as well as better awareness of her space.

"When I come to football, I can see the pitch. I can see my players, I know instinctively where they are. So I have this feeling for it. I always was prepared and I think that came with badminton because [of] the hand and the eye, and you have to move at the same time, and you have to know, 'Where should I put the ball the next time?' I connect this with soccer; it's not really the same but it fits. I was very precise coming to put a ball to another player. I think that's also one of the things you learn: it's inherent to be very exact."

By the time Borjesson was Sweden captain, the Swedish domestic league was also improving, with her club scheduling up to five training sessions a week during the winter off-season, stepping it down during the summer months when the season began and matches were added to the timetable. However, there was one notable problem for players as they moved from the domestic game to international competition: the restrictions that European governing body UEFA put on the women's game. Usually women would play with a standard-sized ball, a number five; in European competition they were given a smaller ball, a number four, as well as a seventy-minute match rather than the usual ninety minutes.

"We had to adjust ourselves when we came to the national team, start to get used to the smaller ball," recalled Borjesson. "It also makes a difference on the foot and on the knee and how to shoot and everything."

Borjesson had been involved in a brand's advertising campaign during the 2022 Women's Euros, along with Carol Thomas, her English counterpart from 1984. The two had not met in nearly forty years, and they finally got the opportunity during the tournament. Thomas's husband Alan had brought the pennant the two captains had exchanged ahead of kick-off at Kenilworth Road, and as soon as she saw it, Borjesson began to cry.

"It was very emotional, and it still is, because that time in '84, we didn't have the time to speak to each other. It's so little [the time they had together]. We didn't know each other. We [played] two games and never saw each other again."

After a fine career in two sports, that 1984 European win remained Borjesson's proudest achievement.

"I know for some people it's not a big thing, but for us, it was. Really, it was the best you can do at that moment, and you can't forget that – sometimes it just has to start, doesn't it? If we hadn't had that game, the things we did before, then maybe we wouldn't have been here. I saw the [Women's FA] Cup final [at Wembley in 2023, which sold out] – it's lovely, isn't it? It's so very nice to be part of it."

Of course, since 1984, and after Sue Lopez's time as international officer, the FA had taken the England team fully within its remit, and slowly worked their way to creating a full-time professional league, intended to improve the talent pool available to the national team's manager. Training time for full-time professionals was no longer a problem in England. The obstacles presented themselves just a little way down the pyramid, as clubs tried to balance their ambitions with their budget and the commitments of their players, just as the England set-up had had to do back in 1972.

A two-time Women's FA Cup winner, Leanne Duffy had enjoyed a fine two-decade playing career with Wigan, Liverpool, and Everton. She had moved into coaching, where she had led Liverpool Feds to promotion to the FA Women's National League Premier Division North, the third tier. Some clubs in that league had access to a lot of resources, which contrasted with Feds, who since their foundation in 1991 had been an independent club for girls and women, except for a three-year link-up with Marshalls FC. Duffy's first team trained twice a week, on a Tuesday and a Thursday, at a football hub in Liverpool; the reserves trained only once.

One of the changes she had made in recent seasons was to bring in more strength and conditioning work in the gym, rather than solely on the pitch. She had noticed since promotion to tier three that most of their opponents were running sessions for non-playing squad members immediately after a match, and if Feds wanted to compete at that level, they had to be doing similar. What Duffy wanted to do was to have two strength and conditioning sessions a week for her first-team squad, but in the third tier of women's football, she did not think it would be possible to get her players to commit to three training days a week, particularly as some of them travelled into Liverpool as it was. Her intent was to have one session on a training day, and then the second in players' own time with some remote guidance so they had a programme to follow.

"It's one of these invisible expectancies really that players are just expected to do it," she said. "It's pretty obvious who does and doesn't, and I'd say if you're playing every week, you probably don't really need to do a lot extra, but if you're not playing every week, they're the ones [who need] to do extra, and it's obvious that some don't."

As a player, Duffy had been on both sides of that equation, and felt engagement with additional fitness and training was sometimes an indicator of an individual's drive.

"We'll have people who don't want to do it, or people who are working and they can't be bothered going to the gym from work, and I understand that, I've been there. That's not too different from when I played – you're expected to do your own [extra training], and if you don't, then ultimately it is on you, and you will suffer because you won't get to the level you need to be at."

Towards the end of Duffy's own playing career, Everton had taken on a strength and conditioning coach who would do running drills at the end of matchday with players who had not got any minutes.

"It was non-negotiable. You had to do it," she said, adding that at Feds she did not want to oversee that kind of training, particularly on matchday, because her priority had to be watching the game and working with the players in the team. She was also very aware that her players were not professionals; though she encouraged a professional attitude, these women had other jobs, and no matter how much they might want to give, sometimes they might not have anything more within them for training or for a match.

"I do try and be understanding, compassionate, empathetic to that, but then it is that player who suffers because they're not at the level they need to be at when they are expected to come into the team. It's a cycle that will just be repeated and repeated. They'll always be a couple of players in your team who will struggle with fitness, who need to do a little bit extra than everybody else, and it's tough on them. That self-awareness is vital, because as a player you need to know where you're at, whether you can actually get away with not training, or not doing an extra session this week, or whether you can never get away with that – some people can never get away with it."

Ironically, the amateur players at tier three were, Duffy thought, being asked to do more than their professional or semi-professional counterparts.

"When you get paid for it, you've not got a choice, and somebody is holding your hand while you're doing it," she agreed with a grin.

The very best male players in the world were spotted as children and welcomed into a set-up that is there to allow them to concentrate only on football, and become the very best they can. With female players' career paths tending to be rather more circuitous, and professional opportunities much more limited, they often have wide-ranging and intriguing life experience alongside their football. Even if a player is given the chance to turn professional, she may well still choose not to; if she has trained for and established herself in a particular career, which is paying the bills, putting that on hiatus for the risky and time-restricted occupation of footballer might not be attractive for her.

However, that means that coaches are presented with players who bring unique skills to their squad and to the training ground. For Jenny Sugarman, when she took over as coach of West Bromwich Albion Women, drawing out the knowledge of her players and encouraging them to actively participate in coaching discussions had been fundamental to her ethos. She had coached at many levels of the game, including a university squad, and when she took over at West Brom had overhauled their training schedule, bringing in another gym-based session and adding video and match analysis time. She knew that with a squad that was not fully professional, asking for more of their time was likely to push some players away, but coaching a club that did have ambitions to move up the pyramid from their current position in the third tier and towards full-time status meant that she had to be clear about the requirements and expectations.

"My expectation is that everyone wants to get better, and the things that I'm doing are going to help you get better so if you're not on board with that, that's OK, but that's not the direction we're going in," she explained. "There's been a lot of change and they're really good with dealing with change generally."

She did not just mean off the pitch, but on the pitch too.

"I believe genuinely that formations are something that you use to get the right people in the right places for different games. But a lot of coaches are like, 'We're just going to play this formation, this is my favourite formation, this is how we play,' and never come away from that. We will, across the season, play pretty much every formation there is, across multiple weeks, and within games players are expected to be able to chop and change based on the game and different personnel. That's something I've always done... so not only are they prepared for change off the pitch, they're prepared for change on the pitch, and I've never heard them blame the formation for a defeat or anything like that, because actually they have the power to change it."

The idea of the coach not being omnipotent may be alien to many in men's football. Indeed, Sugarman had found that her counterparts in the men's game were very surprised at the level of involvement and engagement female players had in meetings and in analysis sessions.

"Our women are teachers, doctors, nurses, project managers, business owners, students, with different professional skills, life skills, that perhaps I'd say one of the professional men's players who is coming to an academy at ten, gone all the way through that system, has never developed different vocational skills that might support them in that environment," she explained.

That was not to say it was easy for a coach to draw opinions out of her players. Sugarman saw her approach as empowering, but acknowledged it was still very unusual even in the women's game, and that she had sometimes found herself in a room filled with an awkward silence as players struggled to form or articulate their views, having never been presented with that opportunity in a football setting previously.

"I expect players to talk. It was painful at the beginning when I introduced video sessions at West Brom, it was really painful for quite a long time!" she said.

"It took a long time for players to get that they had to communicate with each other, they had to have ideas and then share those ideas with the group, and [it's] still [a] work in progress. I think it's something that generally players aren't used to, they're just told what to do.

"My way of working is that they're expected to have an opinion and to share it and to buy in and to respect other people's opinions, and that, I think, gives them the power when things aren't working to try and fix it rather than looking directly to us [the coaches] to fix it for them."

Amy McDonald felt slightly differently about her own philosophy. When she had been unable to get a full-time job in sport, she went to work in social care, which gave her a better insight into psychology. She was appointed as head coach for Rangers, a part-time role, and she tried to be as mindful as possible of her players' external commitments.

"You want to be able to take people on a journey with you," she explained, "but what I found was I was constantly searching for their opinion, I wanted them to be happy, I wanted them to be contented within their environment, and feel confident."

She kept checking in with her squad to gauge their feelings, and came to the realisation that she was never going to make everybody happy. She attributed that to the overwhelming coverage and hype around the men's game.

"Sometimes because of the way that male football's portrayed, a lot of females are searching for something that doesn't exist – like this joy every day that you're playing football and it should be engaging and happy and it's just something that you love to do.

"But it's not that. It's not that in anything."

McDonald loved football, of course, but the point she was making was that succeeding in football required hard work and sacrifice.

"It's your passion but it's enduring and it's difficult and it's hard. The hardest thing about it is to be able to keep consistency and sustainability – how do you stay consistent in your everyday actions? I think that that's something that, yeah, we are still trying to figure out."

She thought that because men's football had a long history of professionalism, male players were used to the way it operated, whereas women were only now getting access to the resources and rigours of even semi-professional, part-time football. By 2023, McDonald had stepped up to the more strategic role of director of women's football, and Rangers were training four days a week. They had access to a physio, a doctor and two sports scientists, but McDonald thought they would easily be able to make use of even more staff.

"It just never seems enough, to be honest," she said, highlighting the work that staff were doing to understand each individual player's needs more deeply, both to support them in their improvement and to help them avoid injury. "We've definitely made the jump [from] amateur to elite."

She smiled as she listed the "daft things" that had changed in recent years. "A big difference is I go to training, the ball is hardly out, whereas when I was the head coach the ball was always out! You got these natural breaks in sessions, running about trying to get as many footballs as possible, but now the ball's always in play."

The players were better and fitter thanks to the increased training time, but that also increased the chasm between the junior section – who played football in addition to their usual schooling – and the first team. One of the innovations Rangers had recently brought in was a day-release programme in partnership with the schools, enabling the best juniors to join the first team for training during the day.

"If [the under-18s] went into a first-team environment full-time, they would break," she explained, but she did have another worry about the younger players, who were reliant on parents being able to drive them to training or to matches, and even on their knowledge of diet and nutrition. "It still feels very like the top end is growing, there's more financial [support], there's more of everything, but still even in top level girls are having to pay to play. It's becoming a middle-class sport because how do parents afford it?"

EDUCATION

Amy McDonald's concerns for her young players would perhaps not be recognised at all in the men's game. The route to professional football for boys has been well established for many years: they get scouted, they sign for a club's academy and they are funnelled through the system to the first team, with access to top-class resources. The players' unions have, in recent times, begun to encourage clubs, parents and players to consider education and a life outside football; if a boy does not get qualifications during his usual school years, there are opportunities for him to study alongside his footballing career too.

For girls with dreams of professional football, the pathways are multiple and varied, and, as McDonald rightly pointed out, often expensive for the individual and their families. Few women have had the chance historically to play for a living, so they have always had to think about what they might do as well as football – not just after they hang their boots up.

When Beth Mead was eighteen, she accepted a place at Teesside University to study a degree in sports development. She had long been around the university as it ran an FA Centre of Excellence, which she had joined at the age of ten until signing for Sunderland at the age of sixteen. As an eighteen-year-old, she was on the verge of making a first-team place her own at Sunderland, promoted to the top tier of English women's football in 2015 at a time when the league was still semi-professional (a term that has been used to cover everything from a situation where a player gets her expenses covered by the club to a part-time contract of employment with significant contact hours meaning she has the chance to train throughout the week). By the time she was twenty, in her final year of her studies, she had already made a name for herself as the league's top scorer, and had received her first call-up to the England senior squad.

Naturally, there was plenty of local media interest around her, and Mead was quick to thank the university for their support and understanding of her ambitions in professional sport. She was part of their elite athlete scheme, which offered physiological and biomechanical assessment along with strength and conditioning provision, physiotherapy, sports psychology and other elements required by any sportsperson who wanted to make it to the top.

She signed for Arsenal in 2017, and featured in England's Women's World Cup campaign in 2019, when they reached the semi-finals. Although she was omitted from the Team GB Olympic squad of 2021, shortly after that disappointment she became the first woman to score a hat-trick at Wembley for England when she struck three times against Northern Ireland in their World Cup qualifying match in October 2021. Her alma mater was, unsurprisingly, very proud of their alumna's achievements, and wondered if they could do something together to help the next generation of female footballers who might want to emulate Mead's achievements. The Beth Mead Scholarship was thus launched in March 2022.

"The way a lot of scholarships are done is that an individual may come forward to the university and have a pot of money that they want to donate and do something in that way," explained Will Jones, Teesside University's head of sport. "So this one was reverse-engineered. We were looking at how we continue to develop the sport offer generally at the university, which has a lot of different facets, and particularly we've got a history of women's football through Beth and through some of the other work that we do.

"The idea was basically just we've got someone like Beth as a graduate, who is doing really well in the women's game. She's playing for Arsenal. She's winning trophies there. She's doing really well. So could we approach her to see if she wanted to be involved in putting a scholarship together?

"What that's then involved is supporting four students, four girls, four female football players. There's a financial contribution that they receive throughout their time in university, and then as well as that they receive a level of support from the university in terms of helping them study and play and potentially replicate Beth's pathway, the things that she had to do when she was studying. If at any point they need any kind of academic flexibility, if they were to be away from the university playing international tournaments, a club opportunity, whatever it may be, then that's built in and that's absolutely, absolutely fine. During their time with us, whilst they are on site, they receive a level of sporting support.

Through our sport science degrees that we do, we've got a good level of academics and practitioners who can deliver sports science support, strength and conditioning support, etc., so they would receive that every week as well as coming to uni to do their studies.

"We approached Beth with that, she really liked the idea – she'd enjoyed her time at uni, she appreciated what the university had done for her in terms of flexibility. She understands the journey of balancing your studies with pursuing your sporting dream."

The university took the lead in putting the scholarship offer together and promoting it, with Mead and her club lending her name and her face along with the Arsenal brand to the launch announcement. Nobody could have anticipated, though, that within six months Mead would be a global superstar. She finished as top scorer at the 2022 UEFA Women's Euro as England lifted their first major senior trophy since 1966 and was named player of the tournament. By the end of the year she was nominated for the Ballon d'Or, the top individual prize in world football, and was named the BBC Sports Personality of the Year. Anyone searching the internet for Mead's name would have come across her links with Teesside University and the scholarship scheme.

"Beth was having a really good domestic season [in 2021/22], and coming to the end of that she had just broken the all-time assist record in the league," said Jones. "So she's going off to the Euros – 'Let's hope she does OK there.' Then obviously it absolutely went crazy, which was brilliant.

"It was just fantastic from our perspective to be able to continue promotion, we were getting people from all over the place tweeting and posting about Beth generally, but then some people latching on to [the scholarship]. I remember [TV commentator and presenter] Jacqui Oatley tweeted about the scholarship and said something about, 'What a brilliant time for Beth to do what she's doing, just as she's launched this.'"

With the number of personal awards Mead was picking up, Jones and his colleagues were looking for further opportunities to promote the scholarship.

"It was a great opportunity anyway for young aspiring female footballers to be able to get a bit of an insight and do a bit of work with a [Women's Super League] player. But now it's 'you could be with the Golden Boot winner, the player of the tournament, nominated for Ballon d'Or' – it just takes the opportunity of what they may get in terms of interacting with Beth to a whole new level."

Although Mead had suffered an anterior cruciate ligament injury in the autumn of 2022, her profile remained high, particularly since the publication of her autobiography *Lioness*, making her a popular guest on mainstream TV and radio, not just sports programmes. The fact that she was still excited to promote tertiary education for female footballers of the highest calibre was, Jones, thought, significant.

"It helps that Beth has not just put her name down because she wants to: she's actually lived the journey itself, which I think is really, really interesting, and great to promote that she's been through that," said Jones. "Given what she's gone on to do, some people might say that given the opportunities she's now going to have commercially within the media, financially, whatever, she probably wouldn't have needed a degree to do anything. At the time, she did the right thing and thought: 'I'd love to be a professional football player. I can make a bit of money out of that. But one, women's football isn't the same as men's football and having a back-up plan for when you come to retire is probably more important, and two, if I don't make it I've still got my degree to fall back on.' Now, she doesn't really need that, but that's not the message that you want!

"I think it's a bit of a balance. We'd love to see that the women's game continue to develop and continue to provide female athletes the opportunity to be able to play full-time, to get paid for that, and then be able to dedicate their all to that profession. That then provides opportunities either during or after that career to [pursue] other sporting opportunities like commercial deals and partnerships and opportunities to become part of the media team: fantastic, and that's great as well.

"But I still think [women's football is] probably at a place where it's appropriate to say, 'Actually, you still need a back-up', [but] then to be honest, you say the same to male counterparts. It's just the system is obviously very different with male football players… they go into that club academy system. They do still do education within those clubs, and the clubs will try all they can to drill into [them] the fact that you need some qualifications, but I guess that transition to then coming to university is a little bit different in the male game… They still get that message constantly drilled into them: 'You need a back-up'. We all know that the vast majority of them won't make it or won't make a lot of money out of professional football, so having that back-up is really important."

Jones also admired Mead's interest in and capacity to talk about topics not directly related to football, talking about LGBTQI+ inclusion in football as well as her own relationships, her concerns around women's and girls' teams playing in white shorts when a player might be on her period, and, following the illness of her mother June, promoting awareness of and research into ovarian cancer.

"Those are things that she didn't have to talk about – she's not getting any kind of financial gain with that – but I think she's quite an open and honest person, she's quite a passionate person, and she is smart enough as well to realise that she's got an opportunity to talk about some of those things and help get those things heard as the Lionesses as a collective squad did with their letter to Downing Street and their desire for PE at school to be redeveloped for girls to have more ability to play football.

"For me, the thing that stood out most [after the Lionesses' Euros victory] was the off-the-field stuff and the legacy they do want to create: the fact they all knew they had a chance to do that, the fact they were all switched on to promote that, and they've been really successful in doing that."

The Beth Mead scholars of the future would not just be talking to a great footballer and getting her advice, Jones thought; they would be talking to someone who was an advocate for causes that meant a lot to her, and who was also on her own journey to understand the sports business and the media. He also hoped that the university as a whole would be able to learn from Mead's experiences.

"We've got a really good reputation and awards for LGBTQ+ work that we've done over the years, both internally with the workforce and externally with students. There's quite a bit of work at the moment [and] projects around making sure that [period] products [are freely available] for students to take away or staff to take away.

"All of those things – I'm really happy they are actually happening and [I'm] keen to promote generally because it fits with everything within the university as well. It's not just purely about, 'Look at Beth, she is a sporting superstar'; actually, it's really nice that there are all these other bits around her that, for me, are just as important."

Bend it Like Beckham was a film that inspired a generation of female footballers. Starring Parminder Nagra (later more celebrated for her role in the American drama ER) and Keira Knightley, shortly to become one of cinema's most sought-after leading ladies, featuring in *Love Actually* and *Pride and Prejudice*, the 2002 movie told the story of Jess and Jules, two teenage girls who love football and dream of becoming professionals. Jules tells Jess that such a wish is possible in the USA, where soccer is primarily a women's sport and the top players are superstars, and both are later offered scholarships to play for and study at Santa Clara University in California. It was a route that plenty of top players from outside the USA had chosen: at the time, England's Kelly Smith and Alex Scott were the best-known examples, but at a time when women's football was still not hugely high profile.

Ten years later, the impact of the film was still being felt.

"I had a friend that said, 'Oh, do you know you can go to America and get a scholarship – the whole *Bend it Like Beckham*? I just thought that was what happens in the movies! So I looked into it and thought, 'That's quite a cool route to go down.'"

Jess Fassnidge had played football all around the Midlands of England. She had spent time at Kidderminster Harriers when they had a regional talent centre for gifted young footballers, but by the time she was considering going to university, she was playing locally in her hometown of Worcester. One of her friends from Kidderminster had suggested she look at a soccer scholarship to the USA, and at the time there were only a handful of companies in the UK which acted as an intermediary between player and potential college. She spoke to a couple of firms, and eventually opted to go with a smaller one, where they got to know their players' personalities and footballing abilities in much more depth. They required a payment upfront so that they could assist her through the process, and though it was a large sum of money for her at the time, she decided this was the route she wanted to pursue.

"The very worst-case scenario is 'I end up not getting a scholarship and stay in the UK and then I'll just go to uni here'," she explained.

The company that Fassnidge signed up with had strong links with Eastern Florida State University, who immediately expressed an interest in offering her a full scholarship for two years, trusting in their long-time collaborator's judgement. This would only give her the first two years of a college-level education, but it would also cover all her tuition and living costs.

"At the time I was like, 'Do I take the first offer?' because you just never know. Then I looked at it and thought after a week, 'You know what? I've got to. It's in Florida. It's a full ride for two years. The worst-case scenario is I go out, I hate it, I'll come home.' If I only get two years, I get two years, but I don't have to pay anything apart from my flights basically. So I thought, 'Let's do it.'"

The agency guided her through all the necessary paperwork, including visas, and put her in touch with another girl from England who was also travelling to Eastern Florida State. Arriving at the airport, Fassnidge found herself second-guessing her decision.

"'Holy crap. What am I doing? Do I definitely want to do this?' Because you talk to your friends and it's like, 'That's epic – like, you're the first person in Worcester to go to the States [on a soccer scholarship] and no one's ever done it before.' Great! And then you think, 'Oh, God, actually I don't know if I can do it.'"

That was where having another English soccer scholar to travel with helped her. The two had not met before arriving at the airport but had exchanged messages, and it calmed their nerves.

"We were both eighteen, very young, but we had one another even though we didn't know each other. We met at the airport, we got on really well, and it was quite nice because we had that instant bond."

Having each other also helped when they arrived in the USA, because they both had an insight into how the other was feeling as they adjusted to their new lives.

They knew before heading out there that they would be required on campus ahead of the start of the semester, because they needed to go through pre-season training. They had lists of what they needed to bring and the types of insurance that were required to live happily, safely and securely in the USA, but they were not quite sure what to expect. Fassnidge was fortunate that her family suggested they all go on something of a reconnaissance mission and look round the university and meet the soccer coach about six months beforehand, so at least she knew a little about what her next two years might look like.

Fassnidge and the other English player shared a room in the university's apartment complex, about a mile from campus ("Nice apartments as well – not like some of the really bad student places you can get," she recalled). They found themselves met with a warm welcome; the team coach met them at the airport, and their new team-mates helped them to integrate quickly, showing them where to shop, where to bank, and where to find anything else they needed.

"You're spending all your time with these people, so you live together, you play football together, you train together, you might have classes together – you're always together. So it's quite nice because they are just the most welcoming people, they were like, 'Right, let's get you sorted.'"

It was not just the day-to-day detail of living in a new country that Fassnidge had to get used to. The Florida climate was unlike anything she had ever experienced before. In England, she had been training one evening a week and playing one match a week; now she was training every single day.

"It's night and day. I had no idea. I had absolutely no idea!" she said. The squad reported for pre-season training in July, and they spent the first few days going through the necessary admin protocols and team meetings before beginning their work on the pitch. They trained three times a day, beginning with a very early morning fitness session. "You do fitness at that time because the heat is so hot in July and August. Then you'd go home for a few hours, eat, sleep, then you'd come back around midday-ish, sometimes later in the afternoon [for the next session], and then you'd go home and then we'd come back in the evening. For the first two weeks it was brutal to get used to that."

Fassnidge had gone from the relative mildness of the English summer and her limited football training regime, reliant on her natural fitness, to essentially a professional set-up. Nothing in her experience could have prepared her for that: playing in thirty-degree heat and having to apply sunblock before taking to the pitch.

"You used to have to weigh in before training," she said, "and then weigh out, obviously [indicating] how much sweat loss you had, and then depending on how much you weighed when you weighed in again later on, if you hadn't kind of taken on the fluids, you wouldn't be able to train. So it was very different than what I was used to, that's for sure."

She adapted to the training requirements quickly, even if she never truly got used to the heat. The number of people that would come and cheer on the team was also a surprise to her; college athletes were the campus rock stars, particularly in a high-profile, popular sport like women's soccer. The majority of the Eastern Florida State squad were from the immediate area, and their families would also come and watch.

"There would be so many people at games, in the stands, and you'd think, 'Oh, my God, I'm not used to this – like, all the other sports [teams] have come!' I just couldn't get over the infrastructure they have in place at college. Then going to experience American football and basketball – there are more people going to watch a college game than are going to watch professional American football, which used to blow my mind. I used to think that it'd be like us in this country having more people going to watch Loughborough [University] Women play than like… Man United or Man City or something, and you think, 'How?' That is so different to our set-up in this country."

Football was all Fassnidge was really thinking about; her studies, she admitted, were secondary. However, she, like all the other student athletes, had to maintain a decent average grade, otherwise they would not be able to compete. It meant that she had to focus on schoolwork whenever she had a spare moment.

"When you're a full-time university student, you're not really full-time, regardless of what country you're in; you have a lot of time to work [a job] or do whatever you want; obviously people go out. You just didn't have that luxury over there, because you're training every single day; you've probably got games, especially between August and December – you're probably playing two games a week because you might play a Friday and a Monday or Thursday and Sunday. You're training every day around that. A lot of the games you have to travel to by coach or possibly plane.

"If you ever had to miss classes [for a match or other sport requirement], you had to touch base with the professors and they would understand; they wouldn't really like it but they would understand that [with] football, you have to go, as long as you're doing the work."

Long coach journeys would see players crammed on to a bus and working on note-taking or typing up an essay; if the squad was away for several days, staff might organise a 'study hall' session where players could come together and work in a classroom environment.

"I particularly struggled at the start with even just adjusting to the way the Americans do it, because obviously university is different. You go from college to university in any country, it's different. That's the whole point. It's higher education."

However, there were some differences she was not expecting: a different referencing system for quoting sources, for example, or tutors who marked her down for spelling words in the English way rather than the American way: "That was strict! It was a huge culture shock."

In the US college system, she did not need to pick one particular subject she wanted to work on for the entirety of her time there.

"It's not like in this country where if I went to uni, I [might] want to do sport science for three or four years, you study [only] sport science and you apply to be on that specific course.

"[In the US], you have preseason…and obviously no one is on campus apart from the athletes, but what they do is they sit you down with an academic advisor and they said, 'What are you interested in?'

"'I don't know! Sport science? Maybe business?'"

All students were required to take classes in English, mathematics and science ("I didn't think I'd be doing that again after high school," noted Fassnidge), but they were provided with a list of what was on offer and got to choose.

"They might say, 'Here's the English classes, you've got to take at least two of these.' You do have some flexibility, so if you know you absolutely hate English language, you know you could probably do all your English classes within the literature side."

Fassnidge's academic requirements were complicated slightly by going to a junior college, meaning she would have to transfer to complete the final two years needed to graduate. She was advised to take all her mandatory courses as quickly as possible, building in some classes in specialisms that she was particularly interested in, so that when she transferred to her new school she would have course credit to take with her plus a good idea of what she wanted to major in.

She ended up transferring to Flagler College for her final two years, and finishing her studies with sports management and business modules. She knew what modules Flagler offered, and in return Flagler knew what they would be getting from Fassnidge: she was a known quantity as she had already played for two years in the USA with Eastern Florida State, which was what was known as a junior college.

"I found a lot of coaches actually do like to get junior college players in because there's not necessarily much of a risk with a junior college player. They've been in the States for two years. They're not really a flight risk. It's not like they're going to bottle it at the airport or get there [and] after two weeks go home because they're homesick. They know what's expected of them in terms of they know how to balance the academics already and they obviously must have done OK."

Junior colleges hosted matches for coaches from the four-year schools to come and watch, but they also filmed plenty of footage of their players, who could then contact other institutions directly if they wanted to. As is often the case in football, many opportunities sprang up from pre-existing personal contact, with coaches speaking to each other about a possible player or a vacant squad place that needed to be filled. Fassnidge benefited from her coach at Eastern Florida State taking some time to talk through her options.

"He'd sit down and be realistic with us," she said. "So if we sat there [and] said, 'I want to get to UCLA,' he'd be like, 'OK, let's be honest, you're probably not going to get a good scholarship at UCLA, you're not going to be good enough, but maybe let's try these routes in these schools, they could be a good fit.'

"People keep tabs on junior colleges. They keep tabs on players. They watch video, they come and watch games. I was lucky that I was at a very good junior college so we'd always make the National Championships, and when you got to the National Championship and the finals, you're guaranteed to get loads of four-year coaches rock up. They'd go to Jeff, our coach: 'Hey, we like this player.'"

Fassnidge spoke to various coaches from many different universities. She had it in the back of her mind that she wanted to play for a team in Division One, the highest level of competition in the National Collegiate Athletic Association (NCAA), because she knew there was a preconception in the USA that the very best players would compete at that level, not lower. However, she also knew that she needed another good financial package from the college she transferred to. Four-year schools were more expensive than junior colleges, and she needed financial support for the next two years to allow her to complete her degree. Flagler College offered her a full scholarship, and although it had not necessarily been top of her wish list initially, she knew she had to accept that place simply for financial reasons. She laughed in retrospect at her initial trepidation about going to Flagler.

"It was actually a fantastic school!" she said. "I went to visit, which is crazy; I think I had about ten schools I was in contact with [about the possibility of transferring] and Flagler were right at the dead bottom! I was like, 'Absolutely not going there!' and then [it's] hilarious how the universe works."

Flagler was just up the coast from Eastern Florida State – about 100 miles or so – so she already had some familiarity with the area, and was used to the climate as far as she could be ("I couldn't truly adapt, because even if I come home for a month I knew I'd always find the first few days a struggle when I went back because the heat is just different with the humidity," she said). She loved her time out there so much that she stayed on after she graduated, getting a visa to enable her to work as an assistant coach, but after her first year she had to think about moving back to England; American businesses were unlikely to take on a British employee as they would then have to sponsor a working visa. Fassnidge struggled back in England.

"You go from being a student athlete where everything is 'Go, go, go!'" she said, "and then all of a sudden you are just dropped. You don't have that element any more. You have to look inside and [be] like, 'What is my worth? That was my identity. What do I now do?'

"The first year I struggled massively. It probably didn't express outwardly, but you struggle because you just don't know how to adapt to not being a student athlete – and then I've been in the States for five years. How do I then adapt back home? So yeah, it was very, very difficult."

Fassnidge had had the opportunity after graduation to go to Sweden and play at a high level there, but she loved her life in Florida so much she opted to stay on. It meant that, although she joined in with some of the training sessions, she did not play competitively during that year. On returning to England, she wanted to find a club that had similarly high standards to those she was used to in the States, which was difficult to come by. Added to that, she was working in Birmingham and had an extensive commute back home to Worcester; she simply did not have the time to train with a squad.

She then took a job at a football recruitment company, helping players like herself to find a college place and holding their
hands through the process – something she described as "eye-
opening". The methods of finding players and matching them
up with institutions had expanded by the time she entered
the industry from the other side. Players could send in a free
assessment online, adding in details about their background,
and Fassnidge and her colleagues would check submissions
daily, setting up calls with potential student athletes.

"If you've got someone that's really good and they've put
that they play for a WSL academy – right, that's hot, we
want to get on that straight away, because the better player
you are, the higher standard you play, the easier it will be to
help that person."

Fassnidge would also present at schools, colleges and
football clubs, collecting contact details from interested
players, and the company would also host several events a
year, one being an annual showcase with coaches from the
States travelling over to watch players in person. She would
also keep an eye on local teams and leagues, approaching
players via social media to ask if they had considered studying in America. Her next step would be matching them with
a college and a coach. Making sure that everyone's football
needs were met – as well as the student's academic needs,
plus their location preferences – could be challenging. She
would ask the player what state they would ideally want
to go to, what kind of climate they would prefer, if they
wanted to attend a private or a public school, how many
people they would like to have on campus along with them.

Then she would search a database of colleges to find suitable institutions that might be a good fit. After that, she would move to discussing with the player what kind of course they might want to pursue.

"That's a big one, because someone might be a very good player, but they might be like, 'I really want to do a specific journalism course,' and then actually the school that's interested [in signing them] only have business, and that's not necessarily right for them. So it is always about finding the right fit, but that becomes a bit of a balancing act. I'd say to the people I worked with, 'You have to rank what's the most important thing.' Of course you want the best school. Most people want to be in Florida or New York, which is amazing, or Los Angeles. Yes, you want the best school academically. Yes, you want your major. Yes, you want the best football team – but if you had to pick out of those...

"So for me, mine was – as bad as it sounds – 'I want to go the best footballing school. Academically I'll do whatever I need to do if it means I can play.' But some people are like, 'I want to do journalism', 'I want to do business', 'I want to do this', which is absolutely fine. It just might mean if that's your focus, with certain schools they might be out of the picture."

Fassnidge's own time in the United States helped with this; she already knew several colleges first-hand, especially those that were in Florida, so she knew what a new student might encounter on campus. However, in such a vast country, there were, of course, some places she had not even heard of, so she combined her personal knowledge with meticulous research, along with getting to know the player.

"You have to get the background of that person first, and you need to know how open they are to certain things, because if they're super closed off and like, 'It has to be Hawaii,' you're going to be like, 'It's probably not going to happen.'"

Fassnidge also offered players an element of pastoral support once they were in the States. The chances were that they would settle in quickly and enjoy their football, meaning that all she really had to do was keep an eye on their social media and give a thumbs-up or a heart to photos and videos. However, occasionally there were issues that required a little more involvement – primarily helping them through homesickness.

"The first few months, when they go out between July, August, I'd normally check in quite a bit because some people don't think they'll get homesick. Some people think they do, and then actually they don't, or they do!" she said. "So I would always check in and made for the company a homesickness document, in terms of 'If you are really struggling, here's some things you can try.' What I would do is occasionally set up Zoom calls because you're a familiar face, and you've been part of that process the whole time, and so I'd be happy to do with that with players that really were struggling – connect them with the right people, check in with their families."

The level of Fassnidge's commitment and how much her work was appreciated by the players was evident by the contact she still had with them, even though she had left the job years previously. Many she stayed in touch with on social media, others sent her Christmas cards, some even went to cheer her on in her own football matches; she had rejoined her hometown club, Worcester City. She had completed a master's in strength and conditioning and performance at the University of Birmingham, and was now working at the University of Worcester as an exercise physiologist. In addition to that, she offered one-to-one football coaching, and ran sessions for people with Parkinson's and other neurological disorders. After stepping away from competitive football for those few years ("part of me kind of bottled it," she admitted, referring to her opportunity to play on the continent), she was now where she felt she should be.

"I believe everything happens for a reason," she concluded.

CLOTHES

There is a photo of England's Debbie Bampton in European Championship qualification action, notorious among women's football historians. The captain is wearing a shirt that looks like it would reach her knees were it not tucked in to her baggy shorts; the sleeve holes look big enough to fit her head through. With the women's kit being provided by the same manufacturers as the men's kit, the women were simply handed the same design, same fit, same cut as their male counterparts. Providing shirts, shorts and even socks designed for female bodies is, even now, less than usual. Indeed, one research paper (led by sport scientist Katrine Okholm Kryger, and also using the input of England captain Leah Williamson) suggests that bespoke women's-fit kits were not available until the 2019 Women's World Cup, and although there is as yet no wide-ranging data on female players' comfort, performance levels or wishes when it comes to kit design, it does seem that socks in particular remain an issue for women; the so-called "unisex" football socks, designed for men, come in sizes that force female players either to choose a size that fits their foot, or a size that fits their leg. This creates the potential for injury, with the foot possibly slipping inside the boot because of the amount of excess material in the sock. With something as apparently simple as a sock causing so many problems, it is no wonder that more complicated bits of sports engineering and more sensitive issues of clothing still cause a problem for female footballers.

Any woman who has ever done exercise – at any level – is most likely aware of how important a well-fitting sports bra is.

Suzie Betts has taken breast protection one step further. The Australian's intention is not to strap breasts down to keep them out of the way during sporting activity, but to shield them from impact and injury. Such an item is not entirely unknown in sport, of course; many players across sports wear shin pads, whether mandatory or a preference. Rugby players and boxers wear head gear to protect their skull. The 'box' in men's cricket has long been a staple of the kit bag, intended for male batters to place inside their trousers, over their groin, and offer some protection for those sensitive areas against a fast bowler sending down a delivery at 100 miles per hour.

Betts's invention came out of her own experience. When she found lumps in her right breast, the surgeon asked her whether she had ever had a trauma to the area. Betts could not remember, and thought it was a strange question. After surgery on both breasts, the conclusion was that the lumps had been caused by an injury incurred when she was younger, possibly when playing sport. She had been a keen netballer and tennis player in her youth, but her daughters were still playing sports with greater physical contact.

"I couldn't get that out of my head. I had two daughters at the time both playing Australian rules and basketball, and I said, 'Do you get hit in the boobs?' and they're like, 'Stupid question. Of course we do.'"

Betts went to the medical literature to find out what people had researched about breast injury, and what was on the market to protect girls and women from it. She was surprised to discover that the famous cricket box was not as safe as popularly believed to be ("it cracks, and I believe sometimes even pinches – it's got its downfalls"), and that it had not been necessarily subject to a great deal of research and testing: "It was about 'Let's just protect the crown jewels'."

That sort of mindset did not exist in women's sport. Betts was focused on her daughters initially and had found some research from college sport, where players had reported breast injury, but they were short-term studies and focused on the immediate issue, such as bruising or missing games. They had not (at that time) been followed up ten or twenty years down the line, meaning there was no evidence about the kind of problem Betts had suffered. She was also saddened to discover that many teenage girls gave up sport after developing breasts, whether that was because of an impact injury causing them pain, or because their breasts were large and they could not find a sports bra to suit them.

She started to develop a prototype protector, and although her planned launch in March 2020 was delayed by the global lockdown due to the Covid-19 pandemic, it gave her more time to look at how this kind of equipment could be used by female players across more sports.

"I realised this is bigger than AFL, this is bigger than basketball, this is actually a global issue, and it was things like soccer that then got brought to my attention. I was worried that girls would avoid chesting the ball [for fear of breast injury] or they'd get a whack [in the breasts]."

Betts remembered watching a match where a female player took a hit to the breasts but did not flinch, then took a hit to the back of the calf and went down injured: "It was like they're taking on what the men do, because that would really hurt, getting it in your boobs, but you're pretending you don't have boobs."

She spoke to some elite female footballers to ask them if they had ever been hit in the breasts during a match and whether some kind of protection would help them.

"They were like, 'I don't know, my boobs have never got hit,' and I said, 'But what about when you were learning?'

"'Oh yeah, maybe they did then.'"

Betts's next stop was the USA, where she pitched her idea for polyethylene breast protectors, aimed at players from grassroots upwards.

"We've got thirty million girls playing soccer worldwide. There's thirty million pairs of shins being protected, but there's thirty million pairs of boobs that aren't being protected. That's a big number."

With her mother, an academic in physiotherapy, Betts researched breast health and how to promote it. Her findings showed that breasts needed to be protected, or "encapsulated" as she described it, in their natural shape.

"What has been available in the market has been

compression. Everything has been about squishing them. Even with a bit of padding, you're still receiving the force impact, which is still going to do damage to your breasts. So we wanted to create something that encapsulated the breasts, kept them in their shape, and something that was easy to adapt with what was already on the market.

"I'm not in apparel, I didn't want to create a new bra. I might be a [bra size] 36C, you might be a 36C, but we're still different shapes. So it was about creating an encapsulation insert that you put into your sports bra or crop top, anywhere, the way you want to wear it."

Betts got girls and women to try out the prototypes across a range of sports, enabling her to tweak the design accordingly and take into consideration some factors she had not even thought about before – including inequalities that existed between men's and women's sport from junior and grass-roots upwards.

"We do a fit calculator, which we have on our website, which takes into consideration the chest measurement, the breast measurement, the boob type – swooping up full, swooping down round – and we really get the right size. We want it snug; we realised that we needed them a bit smaller [rather] than a bit bigger. The ones who may have felt uncomfortable [wearing the inserts] initially, once they started playing, they were like, 'Oh, wow, I just got hit in the chest and I felt nothing.'

"Another thing we noticed, especially here in Australia, was the timetable for girls' sport. My daughter was at a co-ed private school, their [Aussie rules] football team undefeated in four years, the boys' [first team results were] up and down, but the girls always copped the 9 a.m. start: middle of winter, dewy ground, a leather ball that got waterlogged. So they would avoid chest marking, they were getting hit from the bounce coming up, and that was all waiting for the beautiful oval to dry for the guys' 1 p.m. games. So we really noticed then there were the elements coming into it, weather and things like that, which I hadn't even thought about either."

Betts's concept of Boob Armour was born. Her daughters still played sport and both wore the protection their mother had designed. Both wore the inserts next to their skin, the elder placing them in as part of her pre-match dressing ritual before even leaving the house, the younger slipping them in as she would her mouthguard as she ran on to the pitch.

Reviews from other users suggested that having the breast protection there even changed the way women and girls were playing their sports.

"They just feel very confident knowing they're protected and they'll probably do more things that they wouldn't normally do. We did a market research. It was all about confidence, and they said even their coaches had commented on the way they were playing differently."

Betts remained concerned that some coaches and medical staff in sports like football, which had long been male-dominated, were still not realising that female players had different requirements in terms of kit, equipment, and the medical care they received.

"Even the trainers are talking like [women are] small men. They're not realising, so the injuries are not even being asked about. A girl might come off because she got whacked in the boobs and no trainer is saying, 'Hey, do you need ice on your boobs?' So it is an unreported injury.

"My main goal here is to open the conversation, because if it's going to be ignored, we're going to have in twenty years girls all ending up like me – probably worse because I didn't do any of those contact sports, I wasn't getting whacked with an elbow every two seconds."

She wondered whether her idea had been a little ahead of its time, but with the growing visibility of women's sport, and iconic images such as England's Chloe Kelly celebrating scoring the winning goal in the 2022 UEFA Women's Euro final by taking off her shirt, she was hopeful that the necessity of female-specific sporting apparel would become more and more accepted.

"I just want to protect those girls, I want to make sure they don't end up like me," she said.

"We're playing maybe a guys' game but we're playing it in a female way, our way, and it's different. So accept it."

A sports bra is important to stop the breast from moving, which can cause structural damage to the breast, and also create pain. It also has a broader health effect: if a player is moving in one direction with her breast mass moving in the opposite direction, it can make her movement less efficient, or change her breathing frequency, or alter her heart rate, all of which can impinge on performance.

Charly Wright, director and brand manager at bra specialists boobydoo, was never one of the sporty girls at school or university; she trained in drama and started going to the gym and did a spot of weight-training, but she did not think of herself as naturally athletic. When her parents took on boobydoo as part of their business portfolio, they asked their daughter to work there; it was an established concern, running out of a small warehouse unit, sending their products through the post and dropping on to customers' doormats.

"It just completely opened my eyes to this piece of kit that had totally passed me by," she said.

Wright wore one when she was exercising; in fact, she thought that she still had the first one, which her mum had bought her years previously, along with other bits of kit she had picked up because they were labelled "sports bra". Working at boobydoo presented her with a whole range of sporting role models she had never considered previously.

"I got the opportunity to become immersed in women's sport, and my passion for it grew. It was literally just me picking and packing the orders, as it was then a tiny business, and doing the customer service and ordering products for people, and it was very different than it is now, [and] just interacting with women [who spoke about] the challenges that they'd had, and how boobydoo were specialists that had availability of sizes and range and products that really changed their life, and made them more comfortable, made them feel more confident."

boobydoo relied on their team of ambassadors to try out products and give honest feedback on whether the bra did what the manufacturer said it did.

"There are sports bras and these new jazzy buzzwords of 'running ultra bra' and 'mega super bra' and all this," she said wryly, "and you think, 'What does that really mean? And what testing have they done?'

"We have brands that we've stocked for a long time and a few new ones in the mix, but it's really about having that range, because someone might be the same size as someone else but what they want that bra to feel like might be totally different. You might want a front-fastening option, while somebody else wants back fastening, or no fastening. Someone might want to feel compressed; we get a lot of people doing tactile cues. They say, 'I want to feel like that!'"

She clasped her chest tightly. "Or 'I don't want to feel like this!' and '[It looks like I] have four boobs, I want two'. That's where our expertise comes in, to help interpret how a woman wants to feel and then picking her that sports bra that has the features and the construction that's going to give her that feeling that she wants."

Knowing that girls and younger women might not have enough experience of wearing bras to know what might suit them best, boobydoo also offered interactive guides that took them through the elements they needed to think about, but the team also answered individual queries, either virtually or in person.

"It's very conversational, usually, especially if we're face to face with someone. Firstly, we ask what activity they're participating in. If they say football or running, that helps us then define, 'OK, you need a high-impact sports bra.' Impact level's quite an important base rule as the experts to start, [it's] not always something that the woman necessarily knows the difference between. Anything that you're doing where you're running, you're jumping, you're moving dynamically through space, you want to have as much support as you can get to reduce the breast movement."

Showing women the variety of styles on offer was something Wright felt strongly about; she knew from her own experience that women often stuck with a style they had first bought years ago, and they were not aware of other options that might suit them better. However, she also knew that women competing in sport sometimes chose a bra that might not have been her choice as the expert, but which worked for their discipline. She gave the example of a goalkeeper she had spoken to, who wore a crop top rather than a high-impact bra, because she had had so many problems on the pitch with fastenings coming undone or slipping when she was jumping, turning or reaching.

"Sometimes it's not the best bra in terms of support level and impact performance – it's the right bra for the consideration for you playing your game better."

Wright had enjoyed the summer of 2022 not just in footballing terms but, as she put it, "it's once in a blue moon that sports bras become national news." Chloe Kelly scored the winning goal in the Euros final and promptly took off her shirt, whirling it around her head and sprinting across the pitch in delirium, white sports bra on show. Ever the professional, Wright wondered about Kelly's clothing choice: whether she had worn that particular bra because it was provided by the kit supplier or a sponsor, or whether it had been a favourite that she had worn many, many times before.

"It's an individual relationship to the things that you wear closest to your body," she reflected. "It's quite personal."

Professor Joanna Wakefield-Scurr was delighted to see that photo of Kelly's celebration. It was she and her team who had helped the player select that particular sports bra as best for her requirements. More than that, Kelly's ease with removing her shirt and exposing her undergarments made Wakefield-Scurr think that people were beginning to think of the sports bra as a piece of equipment rather than an item of fashion clothing. The media coverage was about Kelly's goal and the team's win – not titillation.

"The majority of [the media coverage] I saw was actually really positive about it and not demeaning the bra or breasts or women's sport," she said.

Breast injury and breast health in women's football are, inevitably, massively under-researched, although there are some helpful studies from other sports, such as Australian rules football and rugby, that have useful findings to inform football's policies and strategies.

"It's a really important area, and one that is under-represented, under-reported, underestimated," said Wakefield-Scurr – otherwise known as the Bra Professor. She and her team had worked with Olympians prior to the Tokyo Games, but even from within the field of breast health there were some unhelpful assumptions about what female athletes required.

"We often get the comment, 'Well, sportswomen don't have breasts,'" she said.

With 150 female Olympians involved in the study, some expected the sample to be entirely made up of women with small breasts simply because they were elite athletes. That was far from the case.

"We had athletes that ranged from an A cup to a double J cup, and from 28 underband to a 44 underband. The range of breast sizes in that population were absolutely huge, and so it's not fair to make that assumption that all athletes have small breasts and it's not a problem for them."

The study found that around half the female athletes had experienced breast pain, and 26 per cent of them reported that it affected the way they competed. For sportswomen of all disciplines, these issues encompassed health and performance.

Those headlines caught the attention of the FA, who got Wakefield-Scurr and her team on board to work with the Lionesses in the lead-up to the 2022 Women's Euros to ensure the players were properly supported with their sports bras. They liaised with the squad's medical staff to educate the players on the importance of breast health, and then did individual assessments and fittings with each of them. Wakefield-Scurr found that some players did not like the idea of wearing a sports bra – a piece of clothing that supported their shape. Instead, they wanted something that would minimise their breasts, and conceal their femaleness in this historically masculine sport.

"What they wanted was to just squash them, hide them. That's so disappointing to hear from my perspective; whatever garment is going to protect the breast and support the health of the breast is the best garment as far as I'm concerned. This is devastating to hear that the most important consideration for them was just that their breasts will be hidden."

Wakefield-Scurr was also concerned about girls and women participating in sport at grassroots level without adequate breast support; she raised similar issues to Suzie Betts's concern about injury causing problems further down the line.

"The movement of the breast we've seen can be a barrier to a lot of women even participating in sport, because they're embarrassed and they don't know what to do about it; it's uncomfortable. We've seen it a lot, and it's a lot more prevalent with younger girls as well: wherever there's a lot of breast movement, they're embarrassed and that can lead to them potentially dropping out of sport.

"The other side I would say is impact and injury to the breast, which in soccer would be related to things like catching the ball on the chest or... direct impacts, whether that's from a ball or another player, an elbow, or a head or whatever it is."

Female footballers, the data suggested, were not using additional protection for the breasts, which Wakefield-Scurr acknowledged was not part of the game's culture, but she thought that in itself was disappointing.

"We shouldn't be just accepting, 'Oh, yeah, you'll get a foot in the breast,'" she said. "We know little about the effect of impact [and] blunt trauma to the breast. We know little about the clinical implications of that. I've been looking into it recently with rugby, and there's been a little bit of research suggesting that impacts to the breast [cause] fat necrosis, a build-up of scar tissue in the breast, and that can have longer-term consequences for breast screening. It shows up as a lump and you feel it as a lump in your breast, and so it can have complications."

There was limited evidence about the implementation of devices such as Boob Armour in football, but Wakefield-Scurr's opinion was that anything that provided support and protection to the breast was better than nothing. Importantly, she thought that such products also raised awareness so players were thinking about their breast health. For a female player of any level seeking a sports bra for the new season, she suggested looking away from compression crop tops, and seeking out sports bras with more structured support.

"Less stretch means more support," she explained. "I would encourage players to look for cup and band size products, because there's more chance you'll be able to find a good fit for you. The sports bras that are sized in small, medium, and large can usually get away with that because they're really stretchy, and because they're really stretchy it means they're not going to provide the support that you probably need on the pitch."

As for girls and younger women who needed more help to navigate the complicated terrain of sports bras and football kit, Wakefield-Scurr and her team had set up a website called Treasure Your Chest. It was a breast and bra educational initiative responding to data they had gathered that suggested that 46 per cent of schoolgirls said that their breasts had an effect on their participation in sport, with 15 per cent saying their breasts were too big for them to even consider doing any sport.

"Puberty really is a milestone, obviously, but there's so much going on hormonally, emotionally and physically, and for girls the breasts are the first visible sign of puberty, and so that's a big change for [them] to deal with," she said, pointing again to the worrying data that suggested that breast movement was one of the contributing factors to the number of teenage girls dropping out of sporting activity. "If we can do something to overcome at least one barrier, maybe that will help a few girls stay in sport."

"My kids have asked for football boots for their birthday next Thursday. Son turns nine and I can buy any pair of boots designed for boys, from £20 upwards. Daughter turns twelve and I'd have to pay £100-plus for boots designed specifically for girls' feet, which she'd soon grow out of."

Broadcaster Jacqui Oatley would surely not have expected some of the shock and outrage triggered by her relatively straightforward tweet in April 2023. She clarified shortly afterwards: "For those asking, yes, there's a difference between male/female bodies and football boots should be designed accordingly in order to minimise risk of injury," adding that she was currently writing while attached to a TENS machine to reduce the pain she suffered with a football-induced knee injury from two decades previously, which had never been properly rehabilitated.

Football boot design might not have caught the attention of many, but properly fitting footwear is essential, particularly in sport. Having a boot that fits correctly will naturally make a player more comfortable, but as Oatley pointed out, it would also reduce injury risk as it would ensure that the leg is aligned correctly, that the player could move properly, and that they were not increasing their likelihood of fatigue. Those issues have all been researched and tailored for male footballers, with women's requirements overlooked. The female foot tends to be shaped slightly differently to that of their male equivalent, requiring perhaps slightly different stud types and positioning; once more, the spectre of the anterior cruciate ligament injury is visible here, as one of the risk factors is the boot getting stuck in the pitch surface, which is more likely with increased surface traction from a shoe designed around men's requirements.

Laura Youngson played football as what she described as "a committed amateur", and always wore children's boots.

"At some point I was like, 'This is weird. I'm an adult female. Why am I having to wear kids' boots to play sport?'"

The ridiculousness of the situation was brought home to her when she took part in Equal Playing Field's world record for the football match played at the highest altitude, at the top of Mount Kilimanjaro, and she got the chance to speak with female professional players and ex-professionals.

"I was like, 'Cool, so you've got these mythical women's boots, because you're professional!'

"'No, we just wear men's and kids' as well.'"

It nudged Youngson to go and explore the medical research that existed on foot structure.

"If our feet are so fundamentally different, why are there not women's football boots? I went on this quest to find them and – 'They just don't exist? What?!'"

Youngson did not have a background in product design nor in footwear. Indeed she had a very varied career, having studied a degree in physics and later worked in diplomacy, in hotel management, in sovereign wealth funds and in sports governance. Nevertheless, she began a journey to create football boots for women, contrasting it with the industry's pre-existing plan: "'Shrink it and pink it' is the standard quote – if you take a men's thing, shrink it, smack pink on, women will love it."

Her background was useful in her new role as entrepreneur, giving her a little bit of insight into a wide range of skills and industries. However, it did not quite prepare her for arguing the business case for female-specific football boots, which she admitted was "ridiculously difficult – you wouldn't do it if you'd known what would happen". Youngson stayed motivated by reminding herself of the demand from players, and that it was not just her who had issues with wearing shoes made for children.

"What transpired is that there are a lot of women that are pretty disgruntled with the equipment that they have, or the choice and the offerings," she said, "and there's also a lot that haven't had the lightbulb moment, so [you] don't know why you're experiencing pain or why you've got this niggle and this barrier [to playing], but there is this underlying frustration."

The experience of feeling a sense of surprise that women needed their own type of football boots was not unusual, but Youngson pointed to the huge range of female-specific running shoes available on the shelves of sports shops; if women need their own shoes for running, why would they not for football?

"I don't know whether it's like a little mind blank about that – we're so used to being marketed to in that way, like, 'Unisex is fine. But hey, for running shoes, you definitely need women's!' There is this disconnect, and I think what we're seeing more and more of is people becoming aware, especially women becoming aware, that actually, 'Maybe I should be thinking about what I'm wearing.'

"The challenge is it just hasn't been widely available to buy. If you look at your own experience of going to sports stores or browsing the Internet, it's really difficult, so then you're just like, 'Whatever, I'll just buy this,' and you just get on with the niggles – 'Oh, my little toe always hurts, it's fine.' For me, having the experience of wearing women's shoes, I then was like, 'This is what it should feel like.'"

Youngson's new boot brand, Ida Sports, started in Australia and manufactured the minimum units possible, which came off the production line just before the Covid-19 pandemic shutdown. That pause in elite sports meant they had additional time to get the boots on the feet of players, and helped them build momentum. That first production run sold out, proving that there was demand for female-specific football boots and that women would buy them.

With players trying out the new boot in competition, it was giving Youngson and her team more data about what female footballers actually needed, adding to the previously limited information that had been collected.

"Our heels are narrower, so in general, where your heel

sits [in a men's boot], you're more likely to get blisters, or it could slop around," she explained, "or you'll buy [a smaller size of] shoes to fit the heel and then your toes get squished in. Your little toe hangs off the edge [of the boot] because the widest point on a woman's foot is in a different place [to men's]. Arch support – women in general have higher arches.

"The big one for me that I find fascinating to research is around how we pressure load. Our hips are slightly further apart, so how we move, our gait is different, so then our stud configuration needs to be different, and the length of the studs, because our body mass is less than men's. You start looking at all these small differences and they add up to a considerably different kind of shoe and shape."

Youngson was aware that the big sports brands were working on their own research with a view to expanding their own provision for female footballers, but felt that Ida Sports' position as a start-up meant they had some advantages, such as nimbleness, thus being able to swerve the levels of bureaucracy to bring a product to market that a bigger company might have. She hoped Ida Sports would be able to increase their range and offer products for other sports as well.

"Honestly, you name the sport, there's probably an underserved market for women," she said.

"We know that internally the other brands face a lot of pushback – 'Oh, it's women's' – whereas that's our whole reason to be, so it makes it a lot easier to work on stuff."

Ida Sports were looking to offer female-specific boots for different football surfaces, but she knew that with the professional tier of women's football still relatively small, not many players could necessarily afford to buy multiple pairs of boots. She acknowledged, though, if a big brand decided to put their marketing and money behind women's football boots, they would likely push Ida Sports out of the market.

"It's incredibly difficult. What I'm excited about is we already changed the industry. So they're starting to make them – any education is good for us. 'Actually, we were wrong, we need to make women's boots!' – and we're going, 'Yeah, we told you so.'"

"As a result of player feedback and the underlying topic of women wanting to move away from wearing white shorts while on their periods, we have decided to implement changes to the products we offer to our female players."

It was a bland enough corporate statement from Puma in the autumn of 2022, but it meant a big change for Manchester City. When they were playing in their famous sky-blue home kit, they would no longer wear white shorts, but burgundy. The club themselves had little more to say, with manager Gareth Taylor adding in a statement via their official website: "I'm sure pretty much everyone would agree we're moving things forward. There's plenty of considerations now for female athletes which are important for them to be the best versions of themselves. There's a much better awareness now, it's more openly talked about, I think it's only good for the girls and for the game as well."

Manchester City were the highest-profile club to have taken such a step, but further down the pyramid other teams had stolen a march on them. Lincoln United's women had already switched to red shorts with their white shirts. Nicknamed The Whites, the introduction of the kit change for the women's team had been relatively straightforward, but it had been a circuitous route to get to that point.

Lincoln United were founded in 1938 as a men's club, and more recently had added a women's team as well as junior teams. However, expanding the provision for people to play had also meant developing the infrastructure, including facilities as basic as placing sanitary bins in the changing rooms.

"Everyone was like, 'Why?' And I was like, 'Because you're going to have women playing. They might be on their periods, they might need to change their tampons!'" Lincoln United board member Laura McWilliams assumed a mock-horrified face and gasped exaggeratedly. "'We can't talk about that!'"

McWilliams was one of the volunteers who had taken on a board position to keep the club running. She was acutely aware of her position as a woman in what had always been a men's club, and when she stepped into her role she was keen to keep as many of the club's old traditions as was feasible.

"Football clubs are very much about identity in a weird way, aren't they? They're very tribal. 'We can't change, it's been like this...' And I think maybe I was a little bit frightened of rocking that boat: new board, young board, woman on the board."

That was one of the reasons she was enthusiastic about a "one club" policy – the same treatment, the same facilities, and the same kit for men and women.

"I'm quite happy to hold my hands up: I made a bit of a mistake," she said. "We're very proud of the fact that we were one of the first in our area [that] our women don't pay to play, shocking as it is; it should just be obvious that they don't, but they never have, and we pay expenses. Women should not be out of pocket to play football. That's the way we've seen it, which is quite unusual."

Other clubs did not have the same policy, and it inevitably resulted in gossip about the way Lincoln United were running and how much money they had at their disposal. McWilliams, though, was at pains to point out that the club were supported by sponsors but were by no means rich, or trying to buy success. She wanted to make it clear that it was simply a case of ensuring that both their senior teams were treated equally.

The players really appreciated the board's support for the women's team. Many of the more experienced players had been at clubs where women's football was well down the list of priorities.

"I've played for many football clubs," said captain Chloe Hodgson, "but there is no club quite like Lincoln United when it comes to the equality and the respect they have for the women's team. I think we're almost a little bit snobby when it comes to football because of how well they treat us and how much of a voice we have. We go to other places and you go in the toilets and there won't be bins because it's a male-dominant club – very common. We'll be like, 'Laura, there's no sanitary bins in the toilets!' and she'll be fuming, she'll be like, 'Right, I'll email them!'

"To us, that's absolutely ludicrous because Lincoln United do absolutely everything they can for us as a women's team. We are treated as equal as the men and for me it's an absolutely brilliant place to play and a great club to play for. The people are all in it for the right reasons and genuinely care about us as players but as people as well."

But that "one club" policy and an emphasis on equality between the men's team and the women's team did lead to a problem, McWilliams admitted.

"Because I was quite keen to be like 'We're one club'… and they've always been The Whites – Lincoln United are The Whites, they always wear a full white kit – I was like, 'Oh no, we've got to wear the same kits.' I got a bit blinkered by it. 'That's it. It's got to be like that, we've got to keep it. It's all the same then.'"

It was the coaches of the junior girls' teams that broached the subject of kit colour, suggesting that some of the teenagers were uncomfortable playing in white shorts. McWilliams was at first inclined to dismiss the feedback.

"I was like, 'Oh, well, the women's team are OK, they wear cycling shorts,' but then the more I thought about it, the more [I thought], 'I don't think I'm right here.'

"So I started to speak [to] some of the first-team players and they were like, 'Oh, my God. We wanted to bring it up. You do such a great job for us. We didn't want to piss anyone off. We get what you're trying to do. The white shorts are an issue. They're an issue.'"

Player Annie Ward was relatively new to the club, but with years of experience in the game she knew the problems white shorts posed.

"We would be in the boiling heat at the back end of the season, having to play games into May because the season's run over, and yes, players would be wearing cycle shorts, absolutely boiling, because they're on their period. Sounds absolutely mental, doesn't it, trying to hide it?"

Even some of the club's efforts to look after their women's team had created additional problems when it came to the white shorts. The kit would be washed after every match, and laid out for them in the changing room ahead of the next game, which meant that players who had an issue with a leak had had to sneak their shorts into their bag, take them home, and wash them themselves, because they did not want the kit man to see the stain.

McWilliams was shocked, and also slightly disappointed in herself. The more she asked around, the more stories she uncovered: younger girls who had looked for other clubs, or had given up playing altogether, because they did not want to wear white shorts. Perhaps it had not been the only factor, but it was certainly real and relevant. Senior players had genuinely considered pulling out of matches that they really wanted to play in because they were concerned. One player was mortified that she had had to ask for a new pair of shorts mid-game.

"I'm a teacher," said Hodgson, "so I know that [this is a] sort of barrier that girls in my class alone have with PE when they're on their period, and how uncomfortable it makes them feel. From what I heard through people who were talking at the club, it was a lot of barriers for some of the girls, potentially even reasons why they didn't want to play or stop playing. I think for them – I think for everybody, to be fair – you want to feel comfortable when you play football, and particularly as a young girl, you're on your period and you've not had your period very long and it's something that can be really quite difficult and, I can imagine, something that would prevent you from playing."

The solution was easy. The players were asked what colour shorts they wanted to wear; if a team wanted to stick to white, they could, but other colours were an option too. Red was put forward as the most appropriate option, as it was one of the colours in the club crest, and the away kit switched to all green. The men opted to stick with all-white, but the women agreed that from now on they would be The Whites, but in white shirts and red shorts.

"We changed it and, actually, me being me, I've made this decision just after the kit had been ordered [with] the white shorts, and they're not cheap," said McWilliams. "I said to the board, 'We're going to have to pay for these red shorts. We'll have to pay for them ourselves. But I promise you, it'll be really worthwhile in terms of the players that we will retain, that will want to keep playing for us.'"

Several of the teams with teenage girls switched to red shorts, as did even younger age groups, for whom all-white kits had been ridiculously tough to keep clean. McWilliams had been pleased by the club's response and the fans' response to what she called "a good news story", but had been even happier – and slightly surprised – by the reaction from other teams after their announcement of the kit change.

"Our headline was, 'You don't have to wear white to be the Whites'," she said. "We didn't get any negativity whatsoever. Some of the [other] teams...were sharing it, saying what a fantastic thing it was, and I think it really struck a chord locally.

"It's only just being thought about, that, actually, what a barrier wearing white shorts is and why – even myself, as a woman, not even thinking about it because I don't play football... and actually how important it is speak to women and ask them what they want and what they need to play."

"It's one less thing to worry about, isn't it?" said Ward. "There's enough to think about on a game day without having to think about your kit really, in reality. When you first start your period, it's not nice anyway. I know when I was fourteen, fifteen I used to wear two pairs of cycling shorts [under kit] just because of the absolute paranoia, really. If you can remove that, any concern about that whatsoever, all you have to worry about is turning up and playing your best football."

INJURIES

The gender data gap has impacted women's lives since the beginning of history. Sometimes these impacts are minor; sometimes they are huge – with substantial, even life-threatening, physical consequences. Feminist writer and campaigner Caroline Criado Perez highlighted this in her tour-de-force polemic *Invisible Women*, in which she argues that the gender data gap is rarely malicious, or intentional, but simply reflects a world in which 'male' is assigned as the 'default human', and female experience is not considered. She points out that the Swedish city of Malmö examined the issues with its data collection about the usage of public spaces, and discovered that girls' sports received less funding; they concluded that investing in girls' sport could improve girls' and women's mental health as well as reduce the risk of the brittle bone condition osteoporosis later in their lives. Significantly for the physiology of the female footballer, she highlights that women's reports of musculoskeletal pain are treated with a degree of scorn; that there is a developing body of research that suggests that pain systems and immune systems operate differently in women and men; and that health apps are only now beginning to consider how to gather useful data about the menstrual cycle and its huge variations between every individual woman.

Possibly the biggest physical concern for women's football anywhere in the world is the anterior cruciate ligament – a knee injury that has become more and more high profile, and the occurrence of which women's football fans were finding themselves able to identify on sight, with the typical presentation of a leg apparently collapsing under the weight of an aerial landing, or a foot remaining stuck in the ground while the body continued to move, the knee hyperextending. It has long been established that women are many times more prone to ACL injury than men, and although every high-profile occurrence has led to more calls for greater research, many risk factors had good evidence behind them. Some were physical: the female body is "quad dominant", i.e. it has more strength in the quadriceps on top of the leg than in the hamstring at the back, meaning the knee is less stable. When landing following a jump, because of factors including wider hips and less strength in the glutes, women are more likely to land in increased valgus, which means the knee moves inwards, placing more strain on the ACL. Women are more likely than men to rely heavily on one leg when playing football, and their supporting leg is more prone to an ACL tear.

Some people had put forward more social reasons, suggesting that the male-dominant gym culture had put girls and young women off from the sort of weight training that might have helped them develop stronger hamstrings and greater knee stability alongside their football training. Poor pitches could increase the danger of a boot getting stuck in the turf and the ACL tearing. There was also a growing body of evidence that an individual's menstrual cycle could raise her risk of suffering an ACL injury, although the variations in hormone levels and cycle between women meant it was difficult to extrapolate any theories that could apply to the whole female population.

Unsurprisingly, with women's football getting greater media attention and superstar players being the ones to pick up these injuries, there was panic around whether the number of ACL injuries in the game was increasing in this new era of professional women's football, with players having heavier training and competitive schedules. Without any historical data, it was difficult to be sure. It could well be that in the years prior to professionalism, unable to receive an accurate diagnosis, or unable to access the top-class medical care and rehab resources available to modern players, female players – at all levels – who tore their ACLs simply retired, without fanfare or ceremony.

At the turn of the millennium, the increasing diagnosis of anterior cruciate ligament injuries caught the attention of the Swedish sporting governing bodies. Funding allowed a group of specialist physiotherapists and trainers to create targeted warm-up programmes to reduce these injuries across sports.

This became Knee Control, a Swedish programme which enjoyed significant success when it came to football. Designed as a supplement to a normal training session, to be performed a minimum of twice a week, Knee Control is intended to last for between ten and fifteen minutes. It is also designed to be used from age ten and upwards, meaning that girls start to benefit from it relatively early on, seeing improvements in their movement patterns, their balance, coordination and functional stability, their core muscle strength, their hamstring strength, their landing strength, their ability to change direction – all while keeping the knee under control.

Brought into girls' football in Sweden in 2009, the data suggested a reduction of around two thirds when it came to knee injury. With all licensed footballers in the country covered by the same insurance company, any injuries had to be reported to them, meaning that there was an extensive database. After the Knee Control programme was embedded across the country, it meant it was possible to track its impact against the recorded injuries; for women, the figures suggested, knee injury was reduced by 21 per cent, and cruciate ligament injury specifically by 13 per cent. The report was later translated and made available in English as well.

The woman who led on the programme design for football had a wealth of experience not just in practice but on the pitch herself. Annica Nasmark worked with the Swedish national team as a physiotherapist, but she had been a top-flight player in her own right during the 1980s, representing Hammarby with distinction. Her playing career was ended with a cruciate ligament injury in 1986. First, she picked up a contact injury in an indoor match, and although she knew she had hurt her knee, she did not get a full diagnosis; then in a match she overstretched her knee, slipping on the pitch, with an MRI confirming what she had done. The damage was too extensive to fix with keyhole surgery, so she hung up her boots. Nasmark knew that other players who had suffered similar injuries before the development and perfection of surgical procedures would have retired, just as she did. She also thought that even now players who were outside major cities with specialist knee surgeons might not get the necessary diagnosis and appropriate care.

"When you don't have the special clinics that check it, they can [only] say, 'Yes, we can see on the X-ray, it's no injury, nothing is broken.' But they never check [for ligament damage]. You can't see the ligaments, so they can suggest, 'Take care for one month and then you can start playing again.' So that could happen, even now, that kind of thing."

However, she wanted to stay active and keep up with other physical activities such as running and skiing, and began to think about the kind of exercises that would help strengthen her knees. This additional, personal expertise fed into her contribution to the initial Knee Control programme; it has more recently been extended into the Knee Control Plus programme, with more exercises, enabling coaches and physiotherapists to mix things up a little and keep them more interesting for the players they worked with.

"In my mind, I just think you must do something," she said, "and it's so boring that it happens. There are a lot of young girls – twelve, thirteen, fourteen years old, and they get this kind of injury, and it doesn't matter if you're a really good player or if you're a player that [is] just there to meet friends."

She emphasised that many factors contribute towards a female player's raised risk of cruciate ligament injury, including a family predisposition to it, the way an individual jumps and lands, an individual's muscle mass, their hormone levels, their sleep patterns, or additional stress in their lives, such as moving house or bereavement. She also mentioned that FIFA's 11+ warm-up programme reduced injury by up to 30 per cent since its introduction in 2006. There had been several studies that examined just how effective injury prevention programmes continued to be in the years following their launch, although some observers questioned whether the programmes needed further updates or amendments for professional female players, and the teenage girls on the elite academy pathway, since their training load was higher than those girls and women on whom the exercises had been initially tested. However, Nasmark herself wondered whether the success of such injury prevention programmes had led coaches and players to consider that the problem was solved, and with a degree of misplaced confidence, even complacency, they moved away from the kind of preparation they needed to do in order to maintain a lower level of injury incidences. If injury prevention programmes were not maintained over the course of a season or several seasons, of course the statistics would start to show an increase in injuries again.

"The most important thing is that you do something before the training or the game to check up your body. How is the balance today? How [are] my hamstrings? How is my knee control when I stand on one leg? How can I move and how do I jump and land?

"It's like when you drive away with your car. You need to check some things."

Not only did that short fifteen-minute preparation give a player time to consider their physical condition in terms of any pain or discomfort, it also gave them time to focus on themselves rather than being distracted with thoughts of the upcoming training session or match.

"If you're more tired, or your mind [is] on the game or in training… you're not there, you think other things. It's so easy. Maybe [by doing a warm-up injury prevention programme] you have opportunity to find out that 'Today my body's not ready for training' and you can feel that, yeah, something's going on. But [if] you don't do it, if you do nothing, you just go in the team and do things, you don't know, 'How is it with me today?'"

As Nasmark had highlighted, recovery from physical exertion – training or playing a match – is an important part of a footballer's life at any level, giving the body chance to knit together and strengthen muscle fibres, giving the mind chance to process the learning and put it into practice next time around. For female footballers, though, even at a high level, time away from the pitch has typically not been proper rest, but simply work of a different form.

Chloe Mustaki began playing in her native Ireland with a boys' club, switching to a girls' team when she had to at the age of fourteen. When she went to university to study international commerce, she had the opportunity to spend her third year abroad; with her minor specialism in French, France was the inevitable destination. Mustaki chose the

French university that had the best links with the best football team, heading to Bordeaux and playing for their side at the top of the national second division.

"I didn't do much partying or anything like that," she said with a smile, "but I had an incredible experience of playing against loads of the French and international players who were playing in the league at the time, and other international stars as well. So it was a fantastic season for me to get that exposure from a young age."

After graduation, Mustaki went on to study a master's degree in international management, and for her mandatory internship went to London. She knew that women's football in England was booming, and also knew that top-flight Women's Super League football would not be possible alongside working full-time; she would need to look for a Championship team that trained in the evening. Then West Ham United manager Matt Beard put her in touch with Charlton Athletic, who signed her up, and she moved to London in September 2019 to begin a season that was ultimately truncated in the spring by the outbreak of the Covid-19 pandemic.

"Those seven months were the most gruelling ones of my entire life so far; I will never forget them," she recalled. "I slept about six hours [every night], and I got up at 6.45, 7 a.m., I spent the whole day out of the house so I'd have to pack my bag for the evenings for training, and I'd get home at 11 p.m. at night, I'd shower, and then I'd get into bed at midnight, and then I'd do the whole thing again."

She was spending around three hours every day on public transport as she commuted to a full day's work, two and a half hours of training and back home again. With fixtures on a Sunday, Saturdays were the only days she had to herself, but she could not enjoy them because she was so physically exhausted by that point.

"Every Saturday I felt like I'd been hit by a bus," she said.

In March 2020, Mustaki tore her anterior cruciate ligament. She attributed the injury to her tiredness. She had been called up for an Ireland international camp, and got up at around 4 a.m. to catch a 6 a.m. flight from London to Dublin, where the squad played a friendly against a boys' team ahead of a double-header of competitive matches. In training the day before the first match, she went in for a tackle and suffered the injury.

"Luckily and unluckily, it was just when Covid burst onto the scene, so everyone was moving to working from home anyway, so I decided to stay in Dublin with my family and get the surgery there, and essentially I spent the following two, two and a half years in Ireland," she said. "The company I was working for, the London-based company, allowed me to work full-time from home, and I worked for two and a half years from Dublin while rehabbing and getting back into football. That was also gruelling in its own way, but at least I had a car there so I was able to get around to my [rehab] sessions and my medical appointments, and I didn't have to get the tube, I didn't have to be on my feet. While the timetable was awful as well, I at least saved some time by being able to drive out there. So I wouldn't have really been able to do that in London given the busyness of the city."

Six months after returning from her ACL injury, Mustaki finally made her senior international debut, and a few months after that, she got the opportunity to turn full-time professional at Bristol City, another Championship team.

"The lack of sleep and stress, trying to balance both [work and football], was horrific," she reflected. "You live through your experiences, and I vowed after that [injury and rehab] that I'd never do it again. It was really tough, really tough.

"Luckily now we're at the stage where that's being phased out because women's football is on the rise. Girls are being able to enter into professional football from quite a young age and they don't really have to bridge that gap in their mid-twenties or when they're in full-time working situations, but it does still happen, and it's very, very difficult in those situations."

Deciding to become a full-time professional in her mid-twenties and leaving her established career on hold was difficult, but she felt reassured by having her degrees and some work experience under her belt should she wish to return to corporate life in the future. The benefits of being a full-time professional footballer were, she felt, obvious.

"The main aspect is recovery, so that can be mainly sleep, being able to sleep enough hours to feel recovered, and then being able to go to the pool. You're not rushing off to work or you're not rushing off to go to bed because you're up at 7 a.m.; being able to go to the pool, being able to just really recover and rest, to be able to perform at your best week in week out, whereas when you're dual career, it's just impossible to be one hundred per cent."

"Sorry if this is slightly political with some of what I say!"

Sports scientist Dr Georgie Bruinvels was used to seeing inequalities between men and women embedded in her daily sphere. When she did her degree in physiological sciences, the male body was treated as the standard human body; the female body was mentioned when there was a discussion of hormones or gynaecology. Although she thought this lack of attention to female needs was beginning to change in the educational setting, she felt there was still a tendency to neglect it: "Tick the box, now you've learned about the female athlete!"

Bruinvels had worked across plenty of sports settings, including a collaboration with tennis coach Judy Murray on her programme to encourage more girls into tennis, She Rallies. She had also worked in football at club and international level, and noted the wildly varying levels of knowledge that coaches and players had about women's specific requirements.

"If we consider the circulatory system, even the muscular system, the way we actually move, the way we metabolise food, the way our immune systems work, the way we regulate body temperature: they're all different [to men], and that doesn't mean they're weaker: they're just different."

The focus on the male body was, she thought, giving some coaches – not just in football – entirely the wrong perspective, which manifested itself when they were working with women.

"All research around training stimuluses and loading is centred around what men need, and it's not through ignorance that people are going down that route, it is just that this is all that the textbook is saying," she explained. "I love running, for example, and I've spent a long time with numerous S and C [strength and conditioning] coaches, and I remember them giving me exercises for my posterior chain, my glutes and hamstrings. It was always like, 'Do you feel your glutes [doing this exercise]?' and I'd always be like, 'I don't know what feeling my glutes is!' because a female finds it so much harder to activate the back of their body effectively, the posterior chain."

In football specifically, there were plenty of indicators that women needed different types of training at different intervals than their male counterparts. Bruinvels pointed out that data was suggesting that women actually recovered from overloading quicker than men in terms of inflammation, but not in terms of their metabolic load.

Bruinvels wanted to see clubs and governing bodies collecting more detailed information from players around their menstrual cycle – not just were they on their periods when they incurred an injury.

"What about where you are on your cycle, because actually that's so much more relevant? How long has your cycle been? Has your cycle increased recently?"

There had been some big media headlines on the link between menstrual cycle and anterior cruciate ligament injury, but Bruinvels felt the reporting had not been clear, creating more confusion for players and fans. She had been running an education session for one team, and began a game where each person was asked to stand up if they believed a statement to be true. One of the statements she gave was that it was more likely that a woman would suffer an ACL injury on her period, and lots of players got to their feet.

"I said, 'Well, why do you think that?' They said, 'Because that's when the oestrogen hormone is high.' They know a little bit, but not enough, and that's really polluting, because that's wrong – that's the wrong science. Oestrogen is high in the middle of the cycle."

Bruinvels, though, theorised some women might get injured while on their period because they had more inflammation in their body, or because their sleep cycle was disrupted, or their coordination or reaction times were slightly off – "but," she added, "it's also about not accepting that. What are you going to do about that?"

This was key. Understanding the injuries to which female footballers were more prone was one thing, and something sports scientists were certainly working on, but Bruinvels highlighted it as almost a campaigning opportunity – that 'political' stance she mentioned. Knowing which injuries women were more susceptible to was one thing; understanding why they happened was another; and stopping them from happening was another thing again. Some teams were now collecting data about each player's menstrual cycle, but that was only useful if it was then assessed and applied.

"We're really trying to be proactive, so we know which phase of the menstrual cycle everyone's in and we know what that means and what they need to do about that to support themselves: who needs to recover more, who needs to get treatment," she said. "But everyone has to play – how they get there can be modifiable."

Did that mean collecting blood data from players every day as a necessity? Bruinvels did not think so. "What your hormones are showing – does it actually matter? Is it not more how you respond to it?" she asked, reflecting on a study she had contributed to during the 2019 Women's World Cup, with academic reviewers criticising their lack of collection of daily blood samples from players. Apart from that being almost impossible to do within a professional international team during a major tournament, Bruinvels also questioned whether there was actually any scientific basis to require it. "What we do know, I believe, is that if we monitor females' menstrual cycles over time, we understand what's normal for them, so we know how long their cycle is. We also know that if their cycles get longer or shorter, that's a sign that something's not quite right. We also know what symptoms they typically present with and we try and get them so that they're supported [and] so they're in a regular cycle with really minimal symptoms. If we can't manage their symptoms naturally – so looking at diet, looking at recovery, looking at other ways we can holistically support them – then do they need medical investigation to see if there's endometriosis there or something like that?"

Bruinvels urged sports scientists and those working in football, though, to look at the flip side of this – there would be times within a player's menstrual cycle where she felt particularly energetic and particularly strong, and once that was identified, her training load could be adapted to push her harder.

"Women's health – mental and physical – will advance the game, and I think we need to be understanding this," she said.

Dr Jacky Forsyth, associate professor of exercise physiology at the University of Staffordshire, felt similarly. She had a strong interest in women's sport and exercise; as the co-founder of the Women in Sport and Exercise Academic Network, she aimed to promote research that would ultimately in turn promote women's athletic participation and success.

One of her most striking studies was conducted with colleagues across the continent, a wide-ranging study which asked people involved in women's football about their perceptions of policies and research about menstrual cycles, hormonal contraception and pregnancy. They began with a survey, following it up with focus groups and interviews, and some of the findings were perhaps surprising. As their publication observed, research on the physical impact and implications of exercise and training in women's football was minimal compared to that of men, but there were studies from other sports that could prove useful – for example, as Bruinvels had said, some work that suggested that sporting performance improved at certain phases of the menstrual cycle, and some indications that hormonal contraception could offer some protection against anterior cruciate ligament injury. However, with so many men dominating the decision-making positions in women's football, and with research suggesting that many of them lacked knowledge about some aspects of the menstrual cycle, Forsyth and her colleagues wanted to explore levels of knowledge and awareness of ongoing research on these topics. They concluded that coaches needed to increase their knowledge of the interplay between ovarian hormones and football performance in order to improve their relationship with their player and then to improve the player's own health and wellbeing. Instead of calling on their coaches for support, and in the absence of guidance from governing bodies, female players indicated that they were supporting each other as a group, sharing information about menstrual cycle, hormonal contraception, pregnancy and childcare, which Forsyth and her colleagues feared could lead to the circulation of misinformation.

Forsyth was at pains to point out that the issues were not just with male coaches of female athletes; women's football was simply a space in which increased coach education could improve their relationship with their players, but also help their players to perform better. Just as Bruinvels had also suggested, she wanted data about players' menstrual cycles to be collected more comprehensively and then used in a helpful way.

"It's fair enough tracking it, but nobody's doing anything with the data, so unless there's somebody there that knows what they're doing, what is the point, because nobody's going to change anything or do anything or adapt anything?" she said. "Our next stage of the project is to go in with these best practices that have happened and to go into the club and say, 'Right, this is how you do it, and this is what you should be doing in response.'"

She added with a smile that she had an "agenda".

"Everybody talks about the negative aspects of menstrual cycle," she explained. "I know that's really important. Of course, we have to consider it. But it's sometimes – often – it's the coach's perspective, [who] thinks there's only ever negative things, which there isn't. There's positive things as well. So what can we do to manipulate the menstrual cycle to optimise our performance or training or health? That is the point.

"So if the work was tracking [menstrual cycle] on an individual basis, and you could see, 'Well, actually, I'm better at this at this time. I'm not so good at this,' maybe you could get a pattern of where you can best improve your performance. You know what it's like, when you go out and train, and sometimes you feel awful and you think, 'Why the hell is that?' and it could just be a menstrual cycle-related thing that you don't feel on a good day.

"And then other days, you go, 'Oh, my God, I'm on top, I'm strong, I'm amazing.' So just being able to track that, then you could modify your training, according to that, and I think that's what I feel needs to be done. It's not just ticking a box. It's seeing what you can do in order to optimise your training and performance."

Understanding the bodies of female footballers in more depth would, she thought, be a first step towards dealing with one of the scourges of the women's game, the anterior cruciate ligament injury. In the year leading up to the 2023 Women's World Cup, England players Beth Mead and Leah Williamson both suffered ACL injuries, as did Vivianne Miedema of the Netherlands, Alexia Putellas of Spain, Marie-Antoinette Katoto and Claire Lavogez of France. In total, it was estimated that around thirty women who could have conceivably been in a squad to compete in Australia and New

Zealand were out with the same problem. These were only the elite players; there were hundreds upon hundreds more further down the pyramid, playing at semi-professional or amateur level, without recourse to the same kind of medical care or physiotherapy during the rehabilitation. Clearly, there was an issue, meaning that female footballers of all abilities were at greater risk than their male counterparts. However, that did not mean it was linked solely to women's hormones or their menstrual cycle. Studies had certainly suggested that there was some elevated risk around an increased oestrogen level also creating greater joint laxity, but it was difficult to get enough broad and detailed data that gave a firm indication of when this might happen in the menstrual cycle, or if it would differ between individuals.

"Unless you're monitoring your oestrogen and progesterone every single day it's very difficult to draw conclusions about when this is going to happen for you," she said. "If we had some technology, a wearable technology like you have with the Apple Watches – 'Ooh, my oestrogen is a bit high today!' Maybe that is the future."

Tammy Waine was one of the brightest English talents of her generation. An exciting attacker, during her career she played for Brighton and Hove Albion, Fulham, Lewes and Worthing, among others, achieving international recognition as a teenager.

When she was fifteen, anterior cruciate ligament injuries were barely heard of. Tottenham's mercurial midfielder Paul

Gascoigne had ruptured his by launching himself into a high challenge on Nottingham Forest's Gary Charles in the 1992 FA Cup final. It had been whispered about as a career-threatening injury; other than that, they were rarely discussed. Waine's knee blew up like a balloon the day after one of her matches, and she had to wait to see a physiotherapist on the UK's National Health Service. She was passed from clinic to clinic, and nobody could give her a straight diagnosis. Some years later, she concluded that she had partially torn her knee ligaments then, and they had begun to heal themselves as best they could, leaving evidence of scarring for later investigations to uncover. She returned to action and was just as explosive and impressive as before, earning herself an England call-up. This was in October 1997, in a preliminary match for the 1999 Women's World Cup. Waine was in the squad with the likes of established internationals Pauline Cope, Hope Powell, Kerry Davis and captain Gillian Coultard. The day before the match, Waine was tackled in training and suffered another knee injury.

"I tried to train through it because I was desperate, absolutely desperate," she explained. "All I ever wanted in my life was to get that cap. I couldn't play, ended up being on the bench."

Again, a full diagnosis was not forthcoming. After some rest, Waine played on, and was offered a full football scholarship to Auburn University in the USA. Their women's team competed in the Southeastern Central Conference of collegiate competition, with a very high level of play. This was an exciting opportunity for Waine: few female players had had the chance to play abroad, still less to access the kind of facilities on offer at an American college. Kelly Smith, the England striker and Waine's contemporary, had trodden a similar path and was then getting her college education along with vast amounts of footballing experience at Seton Hall University.

"It was an absolutely incredible experience, the chance to be a professional footballer, really, train every day – it was the kind of thing kids dream of," said Waine, who by her third year was flying, taking advantage of the strength and conditioning support that was still not readily available to players in England.

"I built muscles, got fit and strong. We were twelve games into a season, I scored sixteen goals, number one in the nation in America, I was national player of the week here, I shattered the university record for goals in a season. It was one of those seasons: as a forward, everything you hit just hit the back of the net. It was incredible.

"And then in training, I received the ball, back to goal, unopposed, turned, shot. That was when it was – it was my kicking leg – and I felt this pop, heard a pop. So many people in America at that point had the vivid scar down the front of the knee and it was scary, because every other player seemed to have it. Everyone knew: as soon as I said I heard a pop, it was like, 'Crap. ACL.'

"I was thankful being out there. I got an MRI within two days, confirmed it was a complete rupture. So I ended up having surgery and there it was."

The surgery confirmed that there had been previous injuries to her knee ligaments, which was not exactly unexpected.

Waine struggled to cope. She had been a soccer superstar, and now she faced a long slog of rehabilitation; even though team-mates understood what she was going through, it was a very solitary existence for a very young woman.

"My life just turned on its head. I've gone from the high of number one in the nation, interviews left, right and centre, just this incredible feeling of being unbeatable on the pitch, part of a team, to then suddenly you're in the physio room. There's no one around. Everyone else is going out to training.

"I'm out in a foreign country. I'm only there for football. A lot of the Americans are there because it's paying for their education; for me, it was the flip side, the education was a bonus, I was there for the football, the soccer, and to then not have that…"

She reiterated that in a strange way it was fortunate that the injury happened there and then, with access to a top-class medical team who had experience in dealing with it.

"I am absolutely grateful for the treatment and care that I had, because it was a really challenging ACL recovery and so I ended up having to have a second surgery. I had [the first] surgery in October. I had a second surgery in spring, so March time – I just couldn't bend and straighten it properly."

Waine was having physiotherapy twice a day, and although physically there was progress, she struggled emotionally to acknowledge and accept that she was not going to be playing football for the best part of a year.

"Doing the same repetitive exercises – you wake up from surgery, your quad's gone, you can't bend, just to even lift your leg – it was the hardest thing I've ever gone through. It was really, really challenging. I was trying to study, my grades dropped, because all I wanted to do was play football."

Waine's team-mates, of course, continued their campaign.

"Everyone else goes off. They're playing the games, they've still got the highs of winning games and scoring and suddenly you're not involved in that any more."

Because she was so young at the time, she did not have much life experience, or the resilience an older person might have when facing such a challenge. With the benefit of perspective, Waine had come to understand the way she related to a serious injury as comparable to any other form of grief.

"You've got denial – when you first get your injury, it's like, 'Oh no, it'll be fine. It won't be that bad. I can come back from this.' There is that huge bit of denial.

"You go through that real angry stage. 'Why me? Why now?' I was like, 'Yeah, here we go again.' I've reached the highest, England – I get injured. Rumours were circulating around me potentially going into the pro draft [in the USA] at that point, because I was doing so well out there, having this breakout season, awards left, right and centre. So it was, 'Why me? Why now? Why has this happened again? I'm a good person.' You go through all this absolute anger and frustration. Not that I'd wish it on anyone, but you're like, 'I love football so much. There are other players that don't love it, they're only doing it because it's paying for their education.'

"Then you go through absolute depression. Yeah, I think I was depressed, looking back at it, because the one thing I wanted to do in my life I wasn't able to do. I had support, [but] I didn't have that emotional support. I did get referred to see a sports psychologist at that point because I was really struggling with coming to terms with my injury, and there were bits of it that helped without a doubt."

She had followed that by bargaining with the universe in her head – "If you can, please let me get better. Please can this be over soon? I want to get back to playing. I promise I'll be good." Finally, she arrived at acceptance.

"You finally do accept that you're going to be out for nine months, maybe twelve. Who knows? You start to accept the recovery. You accept the fact that you're going to be doing the same exercises for nine months and it is tedious, it's repetitive."

That cycle through which she had progressed clearly mapped on to the established stages of dealing with grief, and she wished she had had greater emotional support available to her. She had no complaints or concerns at all with the way she had been looked after physically – or indeed the way that the generations of female players after her had been given excellent medical care to fix their ACL tears – but she did question how their mental health was cared for.

"You're part of the WhatsApp group, but you're not really – you can't share any of the banter because you weren't there. They're all going off to games and stuff and sharing the buzz and the excitement, and you're not part of it and you feel completely out on a limb, I'll be honest."

Waine recovered, and returned to England. She signed for Fulham in 2003, one of the league's leading clubs at that time, and moved on to Brighton and Hove Albion the year afterwards, where she spent the next six years before moving to Chichester, then to Lewes and back to Brighton. In 2015, as the FA began to move on their plans for introducing semi-professionalisation to the two top tiers of the women's game, Brighton started to consider their own structure, but Waine by that point was progressing in her off-the-field career and it would not have worked for her. She was in talks to join Tottenham Hotspur when she suffered another ACL injury – this time a partial tear plus a meniscus injury, with the same recovery programme required, just without the surgery. Over a decade on from her injury at college, Waine could not help but review her football career.

"I was not coming to the end of my career," she reflected, "but nearing that age when a lot of players' careers are coming to an end. I was always fit and healthy and determined that I was going to be one of these players that were playing until they were rolling me out on a zimmer!"

It scared her. She sought help from a sports psychologist again, remembering that it had helped a little in the USA, but her fears were not calmed.

"What if I don't come back from this? What if I have to retire from this injury?"

She did not. She recovered, and continued her career with further spells at Chichester, Lewes and Worthing. Signing for Saltdean in 2022, by now in her forties, she tore her ACL again.

"Everyone always used to say, 'Are you playing next season?' It was an ongoing joke – 'One more season!' I was now forty-three years old, but still playing well. I didn't want an injury to dictate when I was going to stop playing, I always wanted it to be in my hands.

"It probably took an injury for me to end playing, because I think I would always have said, 'One more season.'"

In the time between her second and third ACL injuries, Waine's career had changed slightly, and she had been given the opportunity to attend a course as part of her duties as an engagement officer for a local authority. She experienced what she described as "a lightbulb moment" and realised that she enjoyed talking to people, helping them and supporting them. She pursued her introductory counselling qualifications, and started to think of the void she had felt when injured and isolated – perhaps she could fill that for other players in similar situations. When she decided to retire, again she found it difficult to deal with and wondered if she could help others through that transition.

"I still think there's a void in the emotional mental support given to players, especially injuries, but also through retirement. Deciding to retire, it's been really, really hard. This wasn't my choice. It's been forced upon me. I didn't get to say goodbye to the game. I didn't get to have that emotional walk out on the pitch and kick a ball for the last time. It was thrown upon me."

That third ACL injury forcing Waine into retirement did not just take away a leisure activity; it took away a large chunk of her identity.

"I was Tammy the footballer, and everyone knew me as Tammy the footballer. And now I'm just Tammy and I feel it's the one thing I excelled at and suddenly now I haven't got that."

The physical recovery this time round was more straightforward, as she was familiar with the expectations, but the motivation was much more challenging because she knew she would not be returning to playing football at the end of it.

"Football – it was my world. It dictated everything for the week: what I ate, drank, my training regime, even the highs and the lows – if I did something well on Sunday, those highs would feed me throughout the week. You go to bed thinking of the goal you scored or the tackle you made and then to suddenly not have any of that, I felt completely lost.

"The physical [recovery], it was easier in some ways, but harder because the goal, the carrot wasn't there at the end of this one."

Waine was now balancing her day job with volunteering at a bereavement charity alongside her small caseload of counselling clients. She described herself as a person-centred therapist, allowing each person to lead their sessions. Some techniques that worked well for athletes coping with serious injury might include visualisation, she explained: "What's it going to feel like when you put your boots back on for the first time? Talk me through your routine before a game, start to visualise that process. How does it feel? Rather than thinking about all the negative stuff, actually what are some of the positives that we've got to look forward [to]?"

With a lengthy injury lay-off, thinking about returning to play could seem an impossible dream, so Waine recommended acknowledging and celebrating small milestones. A footballer coming back from an ACL injury might return to doing squats in the gym, and manage 40 kg – perhaps half of their previous personal best.

"But actually, flip that around," suggested Waine. "Flipping is a technique we use quite a bit and so do a lot of other therapists. When you first came out of surgery, you couldn't squat at all. You couldn't bend your leg. You were struggling to get ninety degrees' range of motion. Look how far you've come. You're now squatting with 40kg."

An injured player – maybe one early on in their career, maybe with dreams of turning pro or of international recognition – could be beset by negative thoughts that they felt uncomfortable sharing with those usually around them: a parent, a coach, a team-mate. Waine gave some examples: "What if I don't get back to that level again? The fears around that must be really, really heavy; they were playing hard on my mind [after the first ACL injury]. What if I'm not the same player again?

"It's providing a forum where they don't have to be on their positive behaviour around their team-mates or the physio or the manager or the coach. It's providing a place to bring all the worries, the concerns, the fears, and talk them through in a really safe, non-judgemental space with someone that can really relate and empathise with the situation."

Waine also used some cognitive-behavioural therapy (CBT) techniques in her work, helping clients analyse negative thoughts.

"What's the evidence behind those thoughts? Is there any truth in that? 'I'm not going to be the same player' – but what is the truth in that? Or 'what if I don't play again?' OK, well, let's look at the evidence. What's the surgeon said?

"'The surgeon said surgery was amazing, it went perfectly from their point of view.'

"What does the physio say?

"'The physio is saying rehab has been going really well and I'm on form.'

"So when you analyse that negative thought that's come into your head, there's no evidence to say that what you're going through won't mean that you're not going to play again, because all the evidence is saying that you're on track."

Waine pointed out that elite athletes had very little opportunity to explore negative thoughts in the usual course of their career; self-confidence and self-belief were so often viewed as essential. Working through worries via therapy with someone who had been through the same experiences was, she felt, an opportunity that many sportspeople coping with serious injury could benefit from.

"There are so few places where you can be completely honest because we are always taught positive mindset, positive mental attitude – believe that you're the best and go out there and you'll perform," she said. "We're taught not to talk about our weaknesses, our fears; we're taught completely the opposite. Coaches want to see someone that's really mentally strong and mentally tough. Team-mates will probably go, 'Oh, of course you're going to get back and play,' but they don't know that, as much as I don't know, as much as the person going through it doesn't know.

"Those sorts of comments immediately shut down the conversation around fears and anxieties and worries, and they were huge worries, especially the first time I did it – I said, 'If I do it again, I can't go through this again.' It was horrendous. But then the second time came – 'I've got no choice but to get through it.' By the third time you know what to expect.

"I genuinely believe players need a space just to talk about what is going on in their mind, and be completely honest."

That was not to say, of course, that all players would require the same level of support. Waine said that some players who had the same sort of injury as she had suffered did not struggle emotionally and made it through rehab without too much strain. For those who did need extra help, though, finding the right therapist would be another big challenge, and she felt that with her depth of experience both in football and recovering from injury she could offer a different kind of connection than many other therapists.

"If [you've] had therapy, you indirectly in your head [might] think, 'Well, what do you know? You haven't been through it,' whereas I do think my role, training as a counsellor, can really, really help players because I can empathise. I've been there, I've done it, I've worn the T-shirt three times with that, and I've had another serious foot injury. I can completely relate.

"Yes, it's their story. It's their journey. It's not mine, and two ACL injuries are never the same. But the similarities are there: their emotions, I can completely relate to. So I do think I can add a slightly different perspective to a general counsellor [or] therapist that maybe hasn't gone through it and [is] maybe thinking, 'It's just a game' – but it's not just a game to some people."

BODIES

Female footballers may not make millions from their playing contracts, but sponsorship deals can be very lucrative. With more matches being broadcast, players' profiles are being raised, and their presence on social media is almost a necessity – far from the handful of followers they might have had even five or six years ago, top players now draw audiences of hundreds of thousands, and some even take on staff to manage their digital presence and voice.

Allowing that insight into their lives, whether they were sharing candid photos or staged and styled ones, opened female players up for comments and criticism their male counterparts would not get – discussions about their hair, their clothes, their choice or lack of make-up, their tattoos, their muscles, their weight, their level of femininity. Their bodies are not just the tools of their trade, admired for what they can achieve on a football pitch; their bodies are also under scrutiny. From how they pose for a high-fashion photo shoot in a glossy magazine to decisions about having a baby, female footballers have physical considerations men have never even dreamt of.

From 2021 onwards, the NWSL in the USA was rocked by allegations emerging across clubs that coaches shamed players about their weight and appearance as a matter of routine. It has become increasingly clear that such practices have not been isolated to America, with players across the world discussing their own relationship to their body image and their eating habits, and how that has been reinforced or altered by words from people in positions of authority. The term "fat club" for a group of players pinpointed as needing to lose weight has been in common usage, with big names now feeling empowered to speak out; for example, England's most-capped Lioness Fara Williams has spoken about her concern for young players she sees struggling with their diet and their appearance.

Elite athletes experience mental health issues at the same rate as the general population, but elite female athletes experience them at a greater rate than their male equivalents, likely due to some factors that only women experience – sexualisation, for example, or poor injury management due to a lower level of professionalisation, or the absence of some other necessary support structure. Carly Perry, a researcher at the University of Central Lancashire and a former collegiate soccer player in the USA herself, was lead investigator in a study of female footballers in England's top two flights, looking to discover more about how they understood mental health. A total of 115 players completed a questionnaire (just over a fifth of those eligible to do so – around 500 players were contracted in the Women's Super League and the Championship during the 2020/21 season, when this study was carried out), and the results were alarming. 36 per cent of the respondents displayed symptoms of an eating disorder,

11 per cent displayed symptoms of anxiety, and 11 per cent displayed symptoms of depression; if players started matches regularly, they reported significantly fewer symptoms of depression than those who did not.

Perry and her colleagues speculated that the increasing demands placed on elite female footballers could be in turn increasing their anxiety: demands from media outlets, commercial requirements from clubs and sponsors, and fascinatingly fan engagement, which has long been one of the facets of the women's game in England that observers have praised as creating accessibility, drawing a contrast with the men's game, where players are much more remote figures.

Worryingly, the data suggested that 35 per cent of the players were trying to lose weight at the time of completing the questionnaire, with 45 per cent confirming they had tried to lose weight in the previous four weeks – all during the competitive football season. Perry and her colleagues urged more research on this topic, particularly as typical weight-loss behaviours could prove disastrous for elite athletes: undereating, restrictive eating, over-exercising and more could all have a negative impact on performance and cause greater physical and mental health issues down the line.

As the respondents did not seem to recognise their eating habits as disordered, Parry and her colleagues wondered if such behaviour was normalised in their sporting environment, suggesting that athletes were often praised for their dedication to their sport and "sacrificial acts" such as cutting out food.

The study also flagged up something that may be particularly relevant as women's football continues its shift towards full professionalisation in the top tiers – 'part-time' student athletes were at increased risk of reporting disordered eating symptoms, with the researchers wondering if this could be due to the demands of tertiary study balanced with the demands of athletic competition at the highest level, making the players more vulnerable to experiencing mental health issues.

Almost all of the study's participants said that receiving psychological support would have helped them during their football career, with 90 per cent reporting that, and 86 per cent saying they had wanted or needed that kind of help at some point. However, only 28 per cent had got that support from their club, with 38 per cent getting it externally. The fact that half of players reported that psychological support was available at their club may appear to be something of a paradox if they wanted it but were not using it, but Parry and her colleagues wondered if there might be barriers to accessing it, or if the services offered were not the right ones.

After the questionnaire, Parry interviewed twenty-one of the players further about their experiences.

"I just wanted to understand how they understood mental health within the context of women's football: so is it important? Is it talked about? Is it looked after, basically?

"They really wanted it to be a part of the game. It was really important to them to change the narrative around it and it was not only at a personal level but the societal level.

"All the players in the interview study said that they had had wobbles with slight mental health of some sort, which is normal. Most related that to football. I just thought the most interesting thing of that was [that] they didn't want to not talk about mental health, they just felt like they couldn't right now, but it was really important for them to move that conversation forward, which is funny, because I think in the [academic research] literature, the conclusion is 'get athletes to talk about mental health more' – and they actually want to, so what are we doing? Like, how are we constraining them to not be able to right now?"

The disordered eating displayed by female footballers engendered, Parry thought, "an extra layer of shame" as they sought to hide their behaviour and were embarrassed by what they felt was a lack of knowledge about food on their part. There was also an element of enjoying being able to control their food intake in a sport where so much was out of their hands.

"They are shameful for footballers who are supposed to have it all together, and for elite female athletes who are supposed to know how to eat." In her master's research, Parry had looked at disordered eating in soccer players going through ACL injuries, and had found similar reactions. "College players, they were like, 'How am I a division one athlete and I don't know how to eat?' They were mad at themselves for not knowing things right.

"[I told them], 'Well, you've only been taught to eat in relation to soccer, so in these different periods – where you're in off-season, or you're a sub, or you're injured – you've only been taught in terms of [knowing] how to eat for ninety minutes.' They've never been taught for the actual realities of what the game is." If footballers had been trained to feel that they had to 'earn' food as fuel through their physical efforts, if they were not in the starting line-up or they were injured, they may have then felt as if they were not entitled to eat.

"There's a knowledge gap but there's also a control element of, 'Well, I might as well look good.' It makes sense." Parry pointed out that elite female footballers also take on a lot of promotional duties, looking to raise the profile of the women's game with media appearances, and much of that was dependent on how they looked as well. That higher profile also brought with it a new set of anxieties, particularly if they were active on social media.

"It comes from a good place of 'I want to promote the game, I want to be accessible to fans and people, but then how do I strike the balance of taking care of myself whilst doing this?'" Players identified that they felt under increased pressure if they had a strong social media presence.

"They would just say, 'The social media thing's a dangerous game.' A lot of them said that, because they're like, 'You want to help and you want to raise your own profile and you want to raise your club's profile, but then you're opening [yourself] up to getting a lot of abuse back.'"

She had begun to understand the results she had gathered as illustrating a series of tensions that female footballers in England were experiencing. There was a tension in their career, for starters.

"They're supposed to love this career, which they do – they'll all say it, they do love it – but that doesn't mean there's not consequences to doing that career."

Those consequences could include some of the mental health issues the initial questionnaire highlighted, plus a challenge with how they perceived themselves.

"They are playing a sport that demands a certain body image, but the world's asking them for a different one, for a certain physique," said Parry. She had played at a high level in the USA as well as at a good standard in England, and was certainly aware of coaches who had told players they were too fat, or of squads with a so-called 'fat club', with players given a target weight to reach.

"There seems to be a little bit of a difference [between the USA and England], and it's not all right in America, but when talking to the players from England, they literally said, 'When I was playing in America, we at least knew why we were getting weighed.' We got weighed every day after training but it was 'how much water did you lose [through sweat in the heat]?', it wasn't necessarily about weight.

"I think the missing link here is that there is an importance that needs be placed on nutrition, and muscle mass to fat. [But] one, it's individual to each player: I'm no physiologist, but this has to be cracked. Then two, we need to know why. So 'Why am I getting weighed?' and then 'Where is this impacting my performance, and why?' You cannot just weigh players without telling them why you're doing it, or why are we doing the skin fold [test, measuring a player's body fat], or 'what [weight] do we want you at?'

"That was a missing link in the study. They were like, 'We didn't know why we are in fat club', or 'What [weight] was I supposed to be at?'. Those things stick with you, so while we may be doing better, there's some backwards work to do with the players that are still playing that went through that. There's not a fat club as much any more, and we are more aware, which is so good, so we can't criticise that, that's great, but you can't erase the past. You need to now debunk some of this stuff with them – 'what are these different myths that you've heard about X, Y, and Z, and carbs? Let's debunk them together with a proper scientist because that is the message that they heard.'"

"There's perfectionistic tendencies, I think, in most elite humans, let alone athletes, and I think that that was both a blessing and a curse for my career. I'd somehow formulated an idea in my head that being as ripped as possible was the best way for me to be the athlete that I wanted to be. I adopted that idea from a very young age and my behaviour towards food wasn't particularly healthy. Emotionally, no matter what was going on in my life, I've pretty much just turned to that bulimic cycle, but it's a very easy eating disorder to keep a secret. As my career progressed, it was in and out of my life. I wouldn't say it was an absolute constant, but it was certainly a way that I tended to cope with discomfort."

Sally Shipard was the FFA Female Footballer of the Year in 2012, at the age of twenty-five. She had begun her junior career at a local PCYC (Police-Citizens Youth Clubs) team, having first kicked a ball around in her family's back yard in Wagga Wagga, along with her three brothers. She was well used to playing alongside boys, so when she joined the

PCYC team and she was the only girl, it made little difference
to her. By the time she was twelve, she had realised that she
had a real talent for football, and a year later, she got to go
to the 2000 Olympic Games in her home country Australia
and saw the Matildas play. That kickstarted her ambition.

"I was so hungry for it," she said. "My blinders were on
and I was just football-obsessed."

Any teenager deciding they want to pursue a career in professional sport will be – even if unknowingly – demanding a
huge amount of sacrifice and dedication from their parents.
Shipard's parents were supportive, happy to travel the kilome-
tres required for their daughter to be part of the elite set-up.

"I don't have kids myself, but I think to be even registering
to play football year in year out, it's a pretty hefty, hefty fee
for kids in Australia," she said. One of the biggest shows of
support she identified was her parents living separately for
a year when she was fifteen and had been invited to attend
school in Sydney by Matildas coach Alen Stajcic, who had
seen her playing aged twelve for New South Wales under-14s
in a national tournament. "I know [now] that time wasn't
great for my parents either, living apart, but I never knew that
as a fifteen-year-old kid, I just knew that they were showing
the utmost support for this decision that we've made as a
family, that I was going to be shipped off to school. You basically go to these sports high schools in Australia, and sport
becomes a subject so you just get nurtured through all your
other subjects by all the teachers. It's quite a privileged position, really, because you're put up on a pedestal as this elite
athlete and then all of a sudden you can pull so many strings

as a student, which is great at the time, but in hindsight, you probably miss out on a lot of learning opportunities."

Moving from her close community in Wagga Wagga, and away from her father and her brothers, was in retrospect a big challenge for Shipard, one which she thought had impacted her in ways she had not realised at the time.

"Maybe I missed some crucial developmental years as a human," she wondered, "just in terms of my emotional capacity. I turned to football to cope, and developed my eating disorder behaviours around that time as well. So I was hurting deep down, but I just kept on jumping from opportunity to opportunity and I was able to suppress a lot of this kind of uncomfortable emotion and maybe not have my immediate network to turn to. I kept on achieving and achieving; my mental health, I guess, was really quite suppressed in a way which, at the time, maybe just didn't feel like a big enough issue to address because, yeah, I was achieving success. So you'll say, 'Moving away at fifteen? How was it?' It was wonderful at the time, but in hindsight I think it was very difficult."

A teenager around the turn of the millennium, Shipard thought of it as "a time where skinfolds were really apparent"; these elite young women had regular skinfold tests and had their body fat measured. This had been going on for many years, and plenty of players came through it unscathed. The difference was that Shipard had been born, she thought, with an increased likelihood to take all these potential eating disorder triggers slightly closer to heart.

"We'd have to weigh ourselves all the time," she recalled,

without adding whether there was a sport- or health-related reason for those weigh-ins, such as ensuring that they were taking on enough water after training.

"There was an accumulation of triggers, and from what I understand, we're all exposed to them in some way or another; there's just a small percentage of people that take it on very seriously. There was just some comments that were made [by coaches and staff] that weren't directed at me, but I would apply them to my schedule and life and it just became a bit of an obsession, really."

Shipard was thoughtful enough to link that obsessive side of her nature to the gifts that enabled her to succeed as a footballer.

"Would I have been such a good footballer if it wasn't a part of my personality? The perfectionist in me – I don't know if in some ways it was complementary [to being a good footballer] because it made me work harder at such a young age, but then it really kind of unravelled when I was in my early twenties. I [was] just like, 'This is not a way to live.'"

She was also very well aware that if she thought about it too much, she would get caught into a loop of negativity rather than thinking about her many achievements in the game: playing in two Women's World Cups, the 2004 Olympic Games, where she played every minute except eight for the Matildas, winning league titles with Canberra.

"It was just a branch of the overall tree of life. It didn't override my joyful experiences and connection with my teammates – well, it did to a point that I felt like I was just keeping a secret for a lot of it. I think sport has taught me there's certainly more pros than cons in my experience."

Yet she felt that her best football had been at the age of sixteen, at the Olympics, when she had had no expectations of herself, and nobody else had expectations of her either. The big occasions she remembered primarily as a blur prior to her retirement aged twenty-six in 2014, courtesy of a degenerative knee condition ("I retired young but my career started really young, so perhaps my load wasn't managed as best as it could be when I was in my teenage years, but I don't feel any resentment about that, I wouldn't go back and change how I progressed"), and she picked up a microphone intending to give commentary a try.

"I felt obligated to give back because football gave me so much, but in turn, I'm just like, 'This is not filling me up at all.' I watch the big games now and I keep an eye on the likes of Clare Polkinghorne and Sammy Kerr and Em van Egmond because they were all in the team when I was finishing up, I love them and I'm super-chuffed where they've gotten. But it isn't my life any more. So I struggle to think, 'Well, I actually have had an entire career before this one I'm currently in.'"

Shipard's retirement from football was the catalyst for two years of heightened behaviour around her eating disorder. It was not something she spoke about much at the time, describing herself as "a shell of a human" prior to her admission to an intensive program where the aim was, she recalled, "we need to get you back in touch with reality". She had felt lost, and that she did not have a direction to her life without the football that had shaped it for so many years. She thought that perhaps anyone stepping back from something they had pursued at the highest level for so long would find it difficult to understand their own identity without it – whether that was a career in finance, in the media or, like her, in sport.

"No matter how much you convince yourself you've got balance, at the time I think that was a really big struggle for me," she said, "but maybe I was always on the verge of having a little breakdown given that my mental health wasn't great, even whilst I was playing football. I can certainly say life feels richer now with the work that I've done and I'm feeling more accountable to just making a better life for myself, a better internal life."

Shipard remembered a conversation she had had with her psychotherapist at the time of her retirement, during which she expressed her distress at losing the natural highs with which football had provided her.

"She was really quick to point out that football never provided that; that came from inside of me. Football was the vessel for that feeling. I was like, 'What?! So I can actually feel that through something else?' I know that probably sounds pretty logical and obvious, but gosh, it eased my mind, like I just felt weight dropped off my shoulders. For me to even consider that a potential reality was huge, and it was just timed perfectly. Maybe I'd heard that before, but until you're actually in the right headspace to hear a message like that… that was pretty pivotal for me."

Shipard's new life was very quiet and rural. She worked as a carpenter, and performed ceremonies as a celebrant at weekends. She and her partner had bought a cottage in

Candelo, New South Wales, where they lived with their dog, and where they grew their own food.

"Our veggie patch is bigger than our house," she said drily. "It's a pain in the arse, but of an evening, when we sit down to eat the food that we've grown, it's amazing. We've forged a life for ourselves that feels like us."

One of the unexpected plus points of women's football grabbing a higher profile was a new openness and willingness from those within the game to talk about some of the problems that female physiology occasionally posed, not just for its players but for women worldwide. England captain Leah Williamson and Chelsea striker Bethany England and manager Emma Hayes had all spoken about their experiences of endometriosis, for example – a condition in which uterine lining grows outside the uterus, causing pain, usually worse during the sufferer's period, and potential fertility issues. Such problems had, of course, existed for longer than the women's game had been played, but never before had they been discussed with such frankness.

"My periods were horrific forever."

Karen Farley had played for England in the 1980s and 1990s, with a club career primarily in Sweden. She vividly remembered a five-hour coach trip from the south-east coast to Gothenburg when she was laying across the back seat, vomiting, cramping and in severe pain, on her way to play a football match.

"Back in those days, if you were any good, there was no option to not play because there was no one else that was going to come in that was as good as you. Today the squad is deep and there are substitutes on the bench that will come in and do just as an effective game. We didn't have that luxury back then. If you were a decent player, you were going to play whatever happened.

"And it was crippling. It was absolutely crippling."

When Farley was on the pitch, she continued to suffer. She considered herself lucky that she had never played for a team that wore white shorts, because she found herself bleeding through her clothing constantly. If she jumped for an aerial challenge, the impact of landing combined with the heavy menstrual flow could mean a tampon might literally fall out.

"The impact on your game is huge," she said.

Farley had her first child after she had retired from football. When she went for her twelve-week scan, the doctor told her that she would not be having a natural birth, but a planned caesarean. Farley was surprised that such a prediction could be made so early, but it transpired that it was not a prediction but a necessity. She had fibroids blocking the opening of her cervix as well as endometriosis, and it had taken until 2010 for that to be diagnosed. As a teenager, she had been to the GP to ask for help; as a younger woman, she had exploratory surgery to look for the problem, and none were found. She had been offered various painkillers over the years, but she found that she got used to the dose and it made less and less impact.

After giving birth to her son, she went back for a checkup, and her gynaecologist asked her whether she wanted a hysterectomy – the removal of her womb.

"It was the best thing," confirmed Farley. "My life changed the minute I had that hysterectomy. My life changed, because my periods had dominated my life since the age of thirteen and ruined everything."

Farley thought that female players had previously not wanted to speak about periods or gynaecological problems partly because it would have made them seem vulnerable, and partly because it would have played into stereotypes about women – they were less good at their job or their hobby when they were having their periods. When she joined other former England players for a series of celebrations following the 2022 Euros win, she chatted with her old team-mates about the challenges of mid-life and menopause, and reminisced about the limited support they got during their own playing days.

"Can you imagine what we would have been capable of if we'd have had this?" said Farley, referring to the FA's St George's Park facility. "In our generation, we had some fantastic players [who were] literally just getting out of bed in the morning and being a fantastic player. If we'd have had that care into our bodies, the nutrition: just this looking after us when it comes to being a female, when it comes to being a female footballer, because our bodies are different.

"Forget men's football. Look at how we women are built, what our bodies do. There are so many resources out there in ex-players. No one's ever spoken about it. No one's ever discussed it. When you see the girls now and what they're able to do and what they're being given; just imagine that in ten years' time.

"These people that are just starting to gather this research – in ten years' time that research will be worth something."

The idea that a woman should shelve her career ambitions when she starts a family is surely a somewhat old-fashioned one, yet that is still a widely held mindset in the world of professional sport. It might not be explicitly stated, but a female athlete announcing her intentions to take maternity leave can often be interpreted as an implicit retirement announcement; similarly, a female athlete announcing her retirement is frequently assumed to be a precursor to imminent pregnancy news.

In 2014, kinesiologist Michelle Mottola grabbed a few headlines with the suggestion that a female athlete might gain physical and performance benefits in the months after giving birth. Her ribcage would expand during pregnancy, making breathing easier, and her heart chamber capacity would increase, allowing it to hold a larger volume of blood and supplying oxygen to the muscles in a much more effective fashion.

Researcher Nicolas Forstmann and his colleagues looked at the experience of female elite marathon runners returning to competition after pregnancy, and concluded that motherhood itself had no real impact on performance; what made the difference was the age at which motherhood occurred. Having a child during one's sporting career, they surmised, certainly did not mean that one could not return to elite competition and surpass one's previous high standards. However, that is assuming no complications with the pregnancy, the delivery and the recovery; researcher Rachel Selman and her colleagues highlighted potential risks of maternity, including musculoskeletal pain, urinary incontinence, abdominal separation and pelvic organ prolapse.

Essentially, not enough was known about the combination of sports performance and motherhood on a physical level, but even less was known about the infrastructure that was required to enable women to do both. Pregnancy and birth were just the initial stages; a female athlete's entry into the world of motherhood still needed much more consideration, support and understanding. In women's football, with its structures and governance still dominated by men, this is even more the case. Note, for example, the deliberate and striking word choice of one of the most significant research papers published in recent years on this topic – 'The incompatibility of motherhood and professional women's football in England'. Academics Dr Alex Culvin (a former footballer herself) and Dr Ali Bowes knew that their decision to use such an uncompromising word in the title of their article would catch the eye, but they never considered changing it.

"It really was an issue for players to be to be getting pregnant," explained Dr Bowes. "The word choice 'incompatibility' felt like really the only way where Alex and I could actually emphasise the scale of the problem."

Although Bowes and Culvin focused on England, they set it within a context where football was still a shaky career choice for women globally. They quoted the 2017 FIFPro World Player Union report that indicated that half of elite female footballers globally received no pay at all, with almost two thirds of those who did receive money getting less than 600 US dollars per month. Only 18 per cent of female footballers were considered as fully professional according to FIFA regulations, with a written contract and getting paid more than they laid out in expenses. With that all being said, it is perhaps unsurprising that Culvin and Bowes discovered that the women they spoke to had a general lack of understanding of their employment rights, particularly with regard to maternity protections, and that because job security as a footballer was so limited and short-term for women, this had a big impact on their choices about pregnancy, motherhood and early retirement.

That same survey from FIFPro indicated that only two per cent of female footballers worldwide were mothers – an incredibly low number bearing in mind the age demographic of the women playing at top level. Some of the other statistics went some way to describing this apparent anomaly: 47 per cent of respondents said they thought they would have to retire early if they wanted to have a family, 8 per cent of those players who were mothers received maternity pay from either their governing body or their club, and 3 per cent of clubs provided childcare support. All in all, it was not a very conducive sector for women wishing to combine career with family.

Bowes was, however, hopeful that this had started to change. There were notable if limited examples of female footballers returning to play following pregnancy; then Reading and Scotland star Emma Mukandi, nee Mitchell, gave birth to daughter Innes in November 2021, and called on the foot-ball governing bodies to make some changes to the existing policies.

"The policy is you only get fourteen weeks' full pay and then you've got to go back to your work," she said on the *Off the Ball COYGIG* podcast in January 2023.

"Bear in mind our body is our job, who even came up with that? Surely not someone who's played football and had a baby. Is that a man? It had to be a man. A man was definitely involved in that."

Mukandi was the first player to take maternity leave at her club, and hoped her experience would help to improve things for others, including developing childcare facilities at all clubs, not just the biggest ones. Bowes wondered whether football could learn some lessons from other sports, pointing to the likes of Serena Williams and Kim Clijsters who had returned to the top of the WTA tour, winning titles after giving birth.

"There's examples from various sports where there's been a precedent set that actually it is going to be possible to navigate the challenges of motherhood with the chal-lenges of professional sport," she said, although adding the proviso that a team sport presented additional prob-lems when it came to scheduling. "Think of elite run-ners or Serena Williams, [the] tennis player, who can fit training schedules around what they need. That is just not the case in in a team sport. So I think there will con-tinue to be challenges but I do feel more positive about it. The sporting landscape as a whole is starting to look at women as professionals in a much more holistic capacity:

'OK, well, we are going to have working mums.' It's just that work for these people is slightly unusual in terms of playing football, playing sport, but that there has to be the support structure in place to enable women to come back and be successful at that."

The extracts from interviews that Bowes and Culvin chose to include are intriguing, such as this from a senior international: "We're women, some of us are gonna get pregnant, that's how it works. And I just don't think… especially, and I don't wanna disrespect, but in a male environment, they don't expect that."

"Fundamentally, sport is an environment where actually the whole point is you give everything to it," agreed Bowes. "The idea that you might not have given everything to it because you are having a baby and then that's taking time, attention and energy away from the drive to be the best you can be, there's a cultural incompatibility as well, that spans across all women working in sport."

With governing bodies finally stepping in to make provision for footballers' maternity leave, and gathering feedback from players like Mukandi that it still was not the right offer, Bowes expected that it would take a reasonable amount of time to find a policy that offered women the security they required to take maternity leave and return to their job and that supported clubs at all levels to establish the necessary facilities their players would require for their families. The proof of a successful maternity policy would be players availing themselves of it rather than postponing their plans for a family until after their retirement.

"I think it is a couple of years down the line for sure when we're going to know if these proposed positive changes are going to have an impact on whether or not women think that [starting a family] is a possibility for them, but we will see. We will see the living examples, for sure. Watch this space."

"There was no way I could hide not being able to play because there wasn't many people in my position that could have just stepped in," said Lisa Owen, reflecting on how she announced her pregnancy to her club Cardiff City. "So it was like, 'I'm going to have to say something, I can't just fake an injury!' So I spoke to the manager and he was great, to be fair, and then I told all the girls, and they were all super shocked."

'Shock' might seem a strange word to use about a woman in her twenties announcing a pregnancy, but in football – even semi-professional football – it is still relatively unusual.

"Many women, when they're playing football, I don't think they think, 'I can just go and have a baby,' never mind thinking about the support that they would need to have the baby," said Owen. "I don't even think managers think about it. I think they just think, 'Oh, they're going to go off and get pregnant and I don't think they'll come back.'"

Owen was twenty-five when she had her daughter Rori in 2022. She pointed out: "Most people want to start a family around this age. They shouldn't let football stop them. I took nine months out, and then I was back. So it's really doable, and I hope like people like me can show that, and more people think about it."

Owen had been with Cardiff City for nine seasons, so her team-mates knew her well, but were still surprised when she told them that she was having a baby. She knew she would only be out for as long as she had to be, and viewed it as an interruption to her football career, never a possible ending.

"As soon as I told Iain [Darbyshire, the Cardiff City manager], I made it clear from the day I told them: 'I am planning to come back. I don't want to just quit football. I've played since I've been twelve. And I'm only twenty-five now, to give up would be way too early.' I want to play for as long as I can."

Owen herself was surprised at how emotionally challenging she found the absence of football during her pregnancy. She spent the first few weeks continuing to train with the group in non-contact activities, but found herself having to stop earlier than she would have liked as she was suffering from sickness and feeling fatigued. Instead, she turned to YouTube to look up workouts appropriate for pregnancy, just to ensure she was keeping active, not just for her physical health, for her mental health too.

"The whole time, I just couldn't wait to be back," she remembered, recalling an away game that she found incredibly difficult. "I went away with them and I didn't really know whether I should go or not, because I knew I wasn't going to play, I was just going to watch, and it's far to go! I remember watching everyone and just crying because I was so sad that I couldn't play. I just wanted to play, because it's what I'd done for all my life. It was all worth it, don't get me wrong! But not being able to play, it was... yeah, it was quite hard for me."

Fifteen weeks after giving birth, Owen felt she was physically back to her prime. There had been some media attention around how quickly she had returned to action, but it was never her intention to rush back; she felt that she would know when she was ready. She tested herself out by going to a circuits class after a few weeks, and although her stomach muscles felt weak, she felt otherwise fine. She decided to go back to training within a month of giving birth.

"I still felt sharp on the ball. I just didn't feel strong – like if anybody touched me, I'd fall over, I was so weak! But as weeks went on, I found myself getting better and better."

Owen's partner and parents were all supportive of her quick return to football, and sometimes brought baby Rori along to matches, well wrapped up in plenty of layers during the cold weather. Owen also found that she could focus on football without fretting too much about her daughter.

"When I'm in football, I just forget about everything; I just leave being a mam at home. I go in and then I'm with the girls. As soon as I get in the car [to go home], I'm ringing to see if she's all right!

"You just kind of switch off, but when I walked out [at the home match with Rori in the stands], I did look to see if I could see her and, yeah, it is nice."

After her team-mates' confusion when she announced her pregnancy, Owen was delighted that Rori was now practically part of the squad.

"They all love her so much, they're all crazy about her," she said. "They're always asking about how she is and they love it when she comes to games."

Owen even had a photo of her daughter in a replica Cardiff City shirt, a gift from the team.

"They bought her it! It says 'Mam' and number two on the back," she smiled. "It's lush."

She was pleased that she was not the only mother in the Cardiff City team, with two of her team-mates having a baby in the same twelve-month span, and wondered whether their example of family combined with football would encourage others to consider doing the same.

"The girls in my team, they're all around the same age as me, and when they see Rori they're really broody," she said. "They're like, 'Oh, I really want one!' and I'm like, 'What's stopping you?'

"It's true, though – what is stopping you?"

For a very long time, if anyone wanted to know about how football combined with motherhood, there was only one woman to ask – Katie Chapman.

"That was the tough part," she reflected. "Back then, it was only me and trying to fight for anything, when it is only you fighting for it, was really difficult. And I've learned since: unless you're a parent, you don't really understand how it feels to be a parent and what the pressures are and the guilt and all that that comes with it. They don't understand, and I couldn't get my head around it back then. But since I've gone through the years, I'm like, 'You know what? Actually I understand why they don't understand, because you don't understand unless you're a parent.'"

She made her debut for England at the age of eighteen, and graced some of England's most famous women's football clubs, progressing from Millwall Lionesses, to Fulham as they turned professional, to Charlton Athletic, to two spells with Arsenal, a trip across the Atlantic with Chicago Red Stars, and concluding her career as club captain at Chelsea. She was twenty when she had the first of her three children, meaning that as she rose to prominence, she was already balancing her football with being a mother. As a professional player with Fulham – who were at that time taking a huge leap into the unknown by paying their women's team – she was contractually protected as she took maternity leave, and she benefited from an understanding manager. Gaute Haugenes was married to Margunn Haugenes, a professional player herself, and they had started their own family a few years before. It meant he was very understanding when Chapman told him she would be taking maternity leave, and the club's structures meant she was supported throughout.

"I had a physio that put me through a training programme," she said. "I had a doctor that would check on me constantly throughout my pregnancy. There was no pressure after to get back – I'd put a bit of pressure on myself to get myself back fit because I obviously missed playing and I like competing, and my targets were to get myself back fit ready to play again."

The contractual protection and the maternity leave provided by Fulham were both very unusual at the time; indeed, it was only in the 2022/23 season that clubs in the Women's Super League offered anything more than the statutory maternity provisions. Prior to that, there was no mention of pregnancy and maternity in the standard 'Women's Football Contract' given to female footballers. It was an omission that continued to puzzle Chapman, who pointed to the failures of companies in other sectors to offer a welcoming space for mothers and expectant mothers, meaning that they lost talent.

"There's not been many women who have had children and played football, because I think they're terrified," she said. "Why are we so terrified of women having children? [They think] they're not going to come back the same person and yes, you can have complications, and everyone's very, very different. But I relate it to football. Think of an ACL injury. You'll get them back. No matter how long it takes, you'll get them back to full fitness, to where they need to be. Why not with pregnancy? What is the difference? Because we can come back as long as we're supported and we've got the structure around us to help us get back."

For her second two pregnancies, Chapman was semi-professional, and used her knowledge from her first baby to follow a sensible training programme throughout. She continued to train with her team-mates in non-contact sessions up until about six months in, and then did her own gym and swim sessions.

"I used to get looks in the gym from people – 'What are you doing? What are you doing here?' – like it wasn't OK for me to be there," she said. "That used to make me feel really uncomfortable because people didn't understand, like [they thought], 'You probably should be at home, eating for two and sitting on your backside.' No, I shouldn't. I should be continuing to do this, and I'm grateful that I did because I think it allowed me to get back quicker."

However, having children was one of the things that marked her out as different from her team-mates. Chapman enjoyed being able to take her children on the coach to away games with the Arsenal squad, and she thought the other players had enjoyed it too.

"Some of the girls did actually say. 'You know, it's great to have them, because there's a different focus,'" she said, adding that the intensity of competitive football occasionally required a distraction or a relief. "They were allowed on the pitch after games and be involved in celebrations and for me, I'm so proud of that."

Expressing her sense of pride seemed an unusual perspective; after all, seeing small children run around in confetti or wear their father's name on the back of their replica shirts in trophy celebrations is commonplace in the men's Premier League. Chapman and her boys, though, were outliers, and they were not allowed to celebrate together all the time. Rules for some competitions prohibited it, but Chapman thought that as the women's game became higher profile, the authorities realised they had to relax some of those regulations.

"If you turn around and say, 'You see the men taking their kids on the pitch!' they're then going to tell a woman that they can't do it?" she asked rhetorically.

What Chapman really struggled with was the rigours of international camp with England. Under then head coach Hope Powell, competition for places was tough, and the discipline was tight. Chapman's ambivalent feelings about having to leave her children to play for her country caused her great anguish on so many levels; and, once again, she was the only player with children and thus the only one with this particular problem.

"It's always hard, isn't it, as a mother to leave your kids behind?" she said. "The kids tell you, 'Please don't go, mummy, I don't want you to go.' As much as they're proud, they don't want you to go – you're their mum – and obviously miss you."

Help with childcare costs, or provision on site for the children, might have helped Chapman, but she did not even necessarily need the England hierarchy to do anything other than listen to her sympathetically.

"It was just about someone understanding what it was like to be a parent and how that made me feel in terms of going away," she explained. "I was tired of crying every time I left to go to England camp. It was really, really hard. I just wanted someone to understand that, but because there was only me, and no one else had children, it was difficult to speak to anybody about it, or for them to understand how I actually felt. I felt like there was no real support within that [set-up]."

Chapman struggled throughout her time with England, but after she returned to the UK earlier than expected from her spell playing in the USA with Chicago Red Stars in March 2011, she simply did not have the bandwidth to join the upcoming international camp.

"I couldn't get back into my house, because I rented my house out, I had to go and live with my mum. I was trying to get my kids back into school. There was a camp coming up and I remember ringing Hope and saying, 'I can't do it. I can't do it. I'm upside down.'"

Within a few hours, Chapman's central contract with England had been terminated and her retirement from international football had been announced. Four years later, though, she returned to the squad under new coach Mark Sampson. By that time she was a mother of three and captain of Chelsea, and felt her form was as good as ever. When Sampson asked her if she was interested in returning to the England squad, she confirmed that she was, and he welcomed her back, taking her to the 2015 Women's World Cup in Canada. Indeed, she was surprised midway through the tournament with a surprise from her husband and all three boys.

"I felt with him he was a lot more relaxed, it was a lot more family-orientated," she said. "I felt like he had a bit more empathy with me and managed it a little bit better."

Although the stint out in the USA had brought the issues with England to a head, Chapman did not regret her time there. Then a mother of two, she appreciated the fresh challenge on the pitch, but missed her support network, although she had taken care to ensure she still had a home to come back to after the end of her contract.

"I'm grateful that I didn't give up that opportunity, that I went," she said. "The hardest part about it was that I felt quite isolated. I didn't have my family around me. It was just us. But it's a great life for a single person!"

Chapman's determination was evident in the way she played on the pitch, and she channelled that during her pregnancies and then as she balanced football with motherhood.

"I think that not having that support made me grit my teeth: 'You know what, I'll prove you wrong. That's the mindset I had – I will get back to club football, I'll get back to international football. I am good enough to do it."

She felt she had been fortunate in her pregnancies; although she had an emergency C-section with her first, she recovered quickly, which she put down to her own youth, aged twenty at the time.

"It gets harder as you get older, for sure. I noticed the difference between twenty to twenty-six [with the second pregnancy] and then thirty [with the third], and then I noticed the difference in terms of recovery – I actually think the earlier you do it, the easier it is, and the better for your body to recover.

"The haemoglobin in your blood goes up by 50 per cent because you carry more oxygen and I was obviously training on top of that [during pregnancy]. We did a fitness test when I went back for pre-season and I came second [out of the entire squad], six to eight weeks after having the baby."

Chapman was glad to see female players from the next generation starting their families and returning to play, and also admired top athletes from other sports doing the same. She expected that more women would do the same.

"You're seeing these amazing women come back to the highest level after having children, winning medals and competitions. It just changes people's mindsets of it and takes away that fear that once you have had a child, that's your career done. It's not. You just need the help and support around you and the understanding from work colleagues and the business that sometimes it's not always straightforward with kids; you might get a last-minute call to say they're sick. It's having that understanding that sometimes things might be off the cuff. It's just part of being a parent."

VOICE

From its very beginning, women's football and its players have fought to make their voices heard, and fought for equity and equality. As the game has solidified its position on the global stage, more and more players have called for fair treatment and parity with their male counterparts, from resources to remuneration. Even the highest-achieving female national team in the world has felt under-valued and underappreciated by their governing body; the US women's national team spent years embroiled in a legal battle with the US Soccer Federation, with the players alleging that they were paid unequally compared to their male counterparts. Five players from the team – possibly the most well-known ones, Hope Solo, Carli Lloyd, Alex Morgan, Becky Sauerbrunn and Megan Rapinoe – had originally filed a complaint with the Equal Employment Opportunity Commission in 2016, the first step to pursuing a discrimination complaint.

They then filed a lawsuit in March 2019, accusing the USSF of "institutionalised gender discrimination" against them, and highlighting two areas of grievance – equal pay and their working conditions. Football fans' sentiment was firmly on the side of the superstar players; as the USA won the 2019 World Cup final, the chants from the stands morphed from "U-S-A!" to "Equal pay!"

That outrage on behalf of the players increased in March 2020 when a legal filing by the USSF was made public, and people were able to read the USSF's argument that the USA women's national team "do not perform equal work requiring equal skill [and] effort" because "the overall soccer-playing ability required to compete at the senior men's national team level is materially influenced by the level of certain physical attributes such as speed and strength". It was perhaps no surprise that the backlash was so intense that USSF president Carlos Cordeiro resigned in the aftermath.

The major difference between the men's national side and the women's was how their collective bargaining agreements structured their pay. The men were paid to play, and received money only if they were called up to a national team camp, plus more if they played a match. The women's agreement gave sixteen players full-time contracts directly with the USSF on an annual salary of $100,000, paid regardless of whether they were part of a national team camp or if they played a match, and with additional benefits such as parental leave. The other squad members were referred to as "non-contract players" and like the men, only got paid if they were called up.

Win bonuses were the biggest issue. In the very unlikely event that the men's team won the World Cup, each player would receive a bonus of $407,608; the women got only $110,000 each. Even if the men lost a match, they would still get a payment of $5,000, while the women received nothing for a loss. The USSF argued that they had no control over the prize money FIFA paid to federations for the men's and women's World Cups – a huge $38 million to the winners of the men's World Cup in

2018, and $4 million to the women the year after – while the female players argued in response that the different bonuses were in themselves evidence of discrimination.

The dispute was settled in early 2022, with USSF agreeing to pay a sum of $24 million, with $22 million going to the players as a lump sum, and the other $2 million going into an account intended to benefit the national team's players in their post-playing careers and charity work relating to women's and girls' football.

USSF also agreed to provide "an equal rate of pay going forward for the women's and men's national teams in all friendlies and tournaments, including the World Cup". Rather than the women asking to match the figures promised to the men in their collective bargaining agreement, the compromise was to take the unequal sums of money given by FIFA to federations and then splitting them in a form that both the men and the women could accept.

Yet the USA was not the only country riven with disputes. Players all over the world had been fighting their own battles with federations and received very little interest and support. Ada Hegerberg of Norway, for example, one of the world's finest players, the first female winner of the Ballon d'Or (itself not awarded for women's football until 2018), had stepped back from international football after the 2017 European Championships. She said that she wanted the national federation to show a bigger commitment to women's football, and in the years since has starred in her own documentary in which she expanded on some of the issues that concerned her: a lack of facilities for women's football, boys having more and better opportunities to play football than their female counterparts and a lack of respect for top-class elite female footballers. She returned to the national team's fold at the start of 2022, noting then that discussions with the federation's new president Lisa Klaveness had been helpful.

In Spain, fifteen players had withdrawn from selection in 2022, sending emails to the federation (the RFEF) explaining that national team camp was a situation that affected their emotional and physical health. The RFEF hit back with a strong response, saying that they would not be pressured into making any changes to the set-up, least of all to the coaching team, and emphasising that it was not for players to question decisions of the coaches or of the governing body. Indeed. (Spain ultimately won the 2023 Women's World Cup, with only three of those original fifteen players in the squad, and with no sign of their complaints having been investigated, although new captain Olga Carmona assured journalists: "The federation were marvellous. They put in all the conditions to make us champions of the world.")

In a statement released on Twitter in February 2023, the Olympic gold medal-winning players of Canada said their preparations for the upcoming Women's World Cup were "being compromised by Canada Soccer's continued inability to support its national teams", elaborating: "Now that our World Cup is approaching, the Women's National Team players are being told to prepare to perform at a world-class level without the same level of support that was received by the Men's National Team in 2022, and with significant cuts to our program – to simply make do with less... While we continue our preparation for the World Cup with our new budget reality, we've had to cut not only training camp days but full camp windows, cut the number of players and staff invited into camps, significantly limit the already-limited youth teams' activities, all while we continue to face immense uncertainty about compensation." They announced a day later that they would be going on strike, although they reversed that decision following a threat of legal action, and participated in the SheBelieves Cup – training with their shirts on inside out to make it clear they were there under protest. Ahead of their match against the USA in the invitational mini-tournament, Canada wore purple t-shirts with the slogan "Enough is enough", and both sides took to the field with purple tape around their wrists, huddling together with arms around each other in a show of support.

A matter of weeks later, France captain Wendie Renard announced that she would not be playing at the forthcoming Women's World Cup. She explained in a statement that the current set-up for the national team was lacking, and that she needed to step back in order to preserve her own mental health. More followed her lead, while the French federation (the FFF), like their Spanish counterparts, issued a statement acknowledging the players' actions, and reiterating that no individual was bigger than the national team. (By the time the tournament kicked off, Renard had rejoined the squad after a change in management.)

As all these countries grappled with internal problems with the Women's World Cup approaching, players posted supportive messages to each other on social media. Hegerberg tweeted to Renard: "How long will we have to go through these lengths for us to be respected? I'm with you, Wendie, and with everybody else going through the same processes. Time to act."

Then a new voice joined the conversation. Japan's Yuki Nagasato replied to Hegerberg: "I stepped away from the national team seven years ago because of lack of respect from them. But I couldn't speak out at that time. But now time to act, yes and speak louder!"

Nagasato had won honours in Japan and Germany, including the UEFA Women's Champions League with Turbine Potsdam in 2010, and had helped her nation to lift the Women's World Cup in 2011. Two days prior to her Twitter conversation with Hegerberg, Nagasato had posted on her own website a blog that was critical of the coverage the Japanese federation gave to its women's team, pointing out that a player had live-tweeted the first two SheBelieves Cup games to keep fans in touch with what was happening.

"We think that the lack of broadcast this time for the SheBelieves Cup is due to the fact that the federation has not done anything for 12 years to maintain or improve to make our value and also the abilities to compete at the world stage," Nagasato wrote. "We've been seeing lack of promoting our game, and lack of setting up matches in Japan even though WE WON THE WORLD CUP."

Then she took the big step of writing another blog – one which elaborated on her reasons for leaving the national team in 2016 when she was just twenty-eight, describing it as "not the place where I was supposed to be", with "no respect for players as professionals both on and off the field". Notably, she acknowledged her seven subsequent years of silence on the matter, and explained her decision to talk about it now: "I noticed that to be silent doesn't solve the problem." She added that she wanted the Japanese national team to be the most professional environment possible, setting an example for the next generation as well as other countries.

Nagasato had played her club football in the USA since 2017, and her breadth of playing experience globally had given her an insight into what she felt true professionalism should look like. In an email interview for this book, she explained that she thought that players should be encouraged to work hard and play responsibly, understanding the standards they should set for themselves and understanding the limits and capacity of their own bodies.

"There should be room to make decisions by each player based on what they've experienced," she wrote. "This should be something you have experienced at the club team stage, but in women's football in Japan, there is no professional league culture, and there are overwhelmingly few opportunities to learn such things at a club team. Being treated well is not the only way to be treated as a professional. Players and coaching staff are required to work responsibly with the common goal of winning. For example, If you keep making the same mistakes, you'll get fired or you'll not get playing time at the club team. The coaching staff should evaluate the player [accurately], and the player should take it – If you cannot accept [it], you should ask why. But it should be clear and obvious, and should not depend on who you like or dislike. People who work at a professional stage should not make the same mistakes again and again. This is all about mindset and attitude. It is necessary for players and coaches to take responsibility for all mistakes that occur and deal with them from their respective standpoints, because we have responsibilities for the future. By doing so, we should be able to improve and grow together."

Nagasato felt a sense of happiness now she had spoken publicly about the problems she had seen in Japanese women's football, but was concerned that so many national teams were experiencing such big problems despite the increased financial investment and media interest in the sport. She wanted the coaches, backroom staff and administrators of women's football to be just as dedicated and committed to the sport as the players.

"For seven years something was stuck in my mind but it's finally gone," she wrote. "Japanese fans were wondering why I suddenly started not being selected, and I was [frustrated that] I could not explain why. I hope my voice was delivered to people who needed it. I think there are people who had the same experience as me. But unfortunately there are not many people who think the way I think.

"I feel that the women's soccer world is entering a period of great turmoil. It is a big concern that the power of the players is getting too big. We have been fighting many things for a long time."

She also felt sad that her international career had ended so early; even though the record books still had her sitting behind only the great Homare Sawa in the Japanese top goalscorers' charts, she wondered if she could have achieved more. Indeed, she still hoped that one day she might be able to represent her country again.

"I did not expect this to be the end of my national team career," she wrote. "I sacrificed a lot for my future with the national team. There would have been a chance to play two more World Cups, I would have reached 200 games if I continued to play. I still believe that I am good enough to be able to compete on the world stage and I feel that my performance has been getting better in the last seven years. No one has beaten my goalscoring record in the last seven years. Sawa's record is by far the best and will be difficult to beat over the years, but at this point I feel someone should have broken my record of 58 goals in 12 years – and I am always open to going back to the national team if they want."

Ultimately, Nagasato exemplified the dilemma that so many elite international female footballers found themselves in; although they loved playing for their country, they were disturbed and distressed by some of the treatment they still faced, feeling as if they were viewed as lesser and less important than their male counterparts. Players found themselves having to make a crunch decision: to continue with the honour of playing international football and putting up with such working conditions, or to walk away from it for the sake of their own contentment and calm in the knowledge that they were also leaving behind a huge chunk of their potential. Nagasato did feel that women's football was still not as respected as men's football was, but added a swift proviso that this was probably due to the existing economic value of the men's side of the game.

"Few [women's] clubs are economically profitable like [in] men's soccer, and I feel that financial resources [for the women's game] are not sufficient. It is difficult to manage without the support of the football association and relying on rich investors."

Kate Gill completely understood the frustration of the international players who had organised and spoken out against their federations.

"These players for a long time haven't been appreciated by the federations and now they're asking for the investment that historically has been neglected for them the whole time," she said. "They're performing, they're getting results, they're becoming household names, and they're just not getting the respect that they deserve and the dignity in their career is just not there."

Gill, a former Australia captain, was the co-chief executive of the PFA, Professional Footballers Australia. She had previously served on the board as the first female player to take such a position, and took on a staff role at the union after her retirement from football. She admitted that during the early days of her playing career, she would have had no idea what the PFA actually did, mostly because it had been set up to look after male players and had not changed to cater to the needs of its female members.

"They had to go on a journey themselves to transform their governance and their leadership to be able to look after the female players," she explained, "so that happened more towards the back end of my career, and I started to become familiar with the PFA and the work that they did. I also understood the sacrifices that the players that come before me had made to be in the positions that they were in and to allow us to advance our careers through the sport, so when they tapped me on the shoulder to ask if I would be the first female member of the board, essentially, because our board is composed of active players."

She pointed to the example set by her playing predecessors such as Cheryl Salisbury, for many years the most-capped Matilda.

"It just seemed like a no-brainer to me to actually understand how the union works and understand how collective action works as well so that we can bring about change. That education in itself was fantastic, I learnt so much about collectivism and how the business and the organisation works."

When she retired, she took a few months off, and because she had to move off the board comprising a panel of active players, she was approached about taking a leadership role on staff.

"It was up to me to craft it and shape it how I wanted to, and the passion point I had at the time was around domestic players. For a long time, there was no collective bargaining instrument that looked after them and allowed them to be able to stay within the careers in the sport because there was no renumeration protection, no working condition protections, the minimum medical standards were absent, insurance protection wasn't there, so we had a lot of great talent that just couldn't afford to be involved in the game any more. We were losing so many players out of our system because conditions didn't support them."

She worked with those players to understand their biggest issues and how they could be solved, putting forward the goal of a minimum wage, a stable and balanced domestic competition, and increased publicity around that competition.

"We were able to sit down with the federation at the time and say, 'This is what it looks like. This is why you're losing all this talent. We won't be successful internationally unless you start putting the conditions in place.'"

Gill had been introduced to the game by her maternal grandfather, an Englishman and an Everton fan. At the age of four she decided she wanted to play football herself.

"I always thought I was going to play for Everton, but I thought I would play in the men's team!" she said. She played alongside boys until she was sixteen and was picked up by the national elite pathway, funnelling her through to the senior team via the youth squads. Her parents were insistent that she kept up her education at the same time, and she maintained a passion for learning throughout her youth. Then she got the opportunity to go and play in Sweden, initially with AIK in Stockholm, which opened her eyes to the opportunities on offer to female footballers in other countries.

"It was much more professional than what we had in Australia," she said. "At the time you needed somewhere to go so you could have eight to twelve months of football, and you weren't six months here, four months here. Sweden was really interesting because there were a lot of really high-quality players playing over there. People had spoken about how well developed the clubs were. The sentiment also around women's football and football in general when you come from Australia – you're competing with so many different codes, and it doesn't have that kind of national identity that you do when you go to Europe and you realise how big football is over there. So that was fantastic in itself, to be engulfed in that and to get to experience that, and then the league itself was really well developed and the club was great, facilities were good, and that was the place to be at the time."

Packing her bags and moving to the other side of the world was not a troubling decision for Gill. Since the age of sixteen, she had travelled widely with the Australia youth team.

"I never really felt tethered anywhere," she said. "I spent a long part of my life living out of a suitcase in different locations."

That was great for her in her twenties, as she flew between Sweden and Australia, representing various clubs in both countries, but as she moved towards the end of her career, she started to find it tiring and tiresome.

"I was used to being a bit transient and not really having a stable base and just coming and going, but that was what it was at the time, unfortunately," she said. "It wasn't really heard of to stick to a club for a very long time and it was [about] having experiences and opportunities and making the most out of your career because it is very short and precarious and you have to enjoy it while you can."

The precarity of football as a career was brought into sharp relief in 2011, when, aged twenty-six, she suffered an anterior cruciate ligament injury while playing for Linköping in Sweden. It was two months before the Women's World Cup in Germany, and, at the peak of her powers, she had been looking forward to leading the line for the Matildas there. In a league match of no real importance, Gill had begged her coach to let her come on as substitute and get some minutes. One bad tackle later, she heard the snap in her knee, and knew she would not be at the World Cup. It also presented some new decisions for her.

"The hard thing for me at that time was that the medical support that I was offered in Sweden wasn't as good as the care I knew I would get back home. So I had to make the decision to leave the club, but obviously that meant terminating my contract. That was how it was at the time. If I'd stayed and done my rehab with the club there, I could have kept my contract and see what happened, but I knew I would get better medical support back home. So I just went home, got my surgery, rehabbed, reassessed where I was, but I probably lost a little bit of passion after that. It was really hard to get motivated and I didn't want to go back overseas again. I reached [the end of] my tether. I didn't want to be living out of the suitcase anymore, probably because I had twelve months back here [in Australia] around my family and realised, 'Actually, I've missed a lot with them and I really just want to be around them.' Life catches up with you and you'd be like, 'OK, there is more to life than just football.'"

Gill had taken a role as UN goodwill ambassador for the federation's Asian Football against Hunger campaign, and travelled to Vietnam later in 2011 to see how the sustainable food projects there operated. She saw it as a chance to understand how people lived their lives, and to improve them if she could, which she described as something about which she cared deeply.

"I've always wanted to do what's fair and right for people," she said. That opportunity and that reassessment of her life after her serious knee injury put her on the path to her union leadership. As the PFA itself changed, Gill saw potential for female players' voices to be heard, and for the position of women's football to rise, with the league now running independently of the governing body, who led the national team.

"I have so much faith in women's football actually realising its potential and it being given the investment that it needs to do so, and the room and the space that it needs to have its own identity," she said. "I feel like we're starting and we're on that trajectory. I almost feel like the men's game needs to get out of the way."

When Carson Pickett was in her freshman year at Florida State University, she took to wearing long-sleeved jumpers and jackets around campus. The weather was not chilly in Tallahassee, a part of the world with high humidity and sub-tropical temperatures. It was just her way of trying to stop people from looking at her.

Pickett was born without a left hand and forearm. It was the result of amniotic band syndrome, or constriction ring syndrome, a rare occurrence when bits of the amniotic sac – where the embryo is growing – break away and get wrapped around the developing foetus. In Pickett's case, the band tangled itself around her left arm, preventing the forearm and hand from developing.

As she tried to settle in at college, Pickett was adamant that she wanted people to get to know her first, and to be recognised as a good soccer player, rather than simply seen as "the girl with one arm". She also felt vicarious embarrassment for the people she was spending time with, because she knew others would be staring at her arm, making it awkward for everyone.

"Looking back, I wish I didn't do that," she said. "I wish I would have just been happy and proud about my arm, because… people would look at me but maybe they would ask what happened instead [of] just staring at me. I actually appreciate when people do ask questions because I think that they're just intrigued by it: they don't know, they don't have one arm, they probably don't have people in their life that have one arm."

Pickett was a fan of having those kinds of chats. Opposition players had sometimes asked her questions about her limb difference that she had not even considered before, so it was invigorating for her, but she still had regret for the teenager she once was.

"I hid it for a really long time, just hoping people wouldn't think of me any different than a student athlete at Florida State, and they wouldn't look at me, because I just hated when people would stare at my arm," she said.

Throughout her teenage years – hardly a time where any kind of difference is welcomed amongst one's peer group, or where difference makes one feel more comfortable with oneself – Pickett felt like she wanted to prove herself. She wanted respect from other players and from coaches, and she did not want anyone to think she had ever been given anything because of her limb difference.

"I wanted these things to happen through my ability on the field, but then I realised that I do have so much power with my arm, I have so much opportunity to help people understand that there are other people like me out there, because I do get a lot of questions because people just aren't educated about it, it's not their fault, there's just not tons of people with limb difference out there," she said. "So I felt like if I was able to put my arm out there, it would start conversations and it would be open for people to ask questions, whereas before I was hiding it on social media. Maybe they thought that it was a little awkward to ask questions because I wasn't proud of having one arm. By putting it on social media, it did open dialogue and conversation, and I hope that it starts it everywhere, and I hope that it can be something that's not awkward or uncomfortable to talk about."

The social media post that changed Pickett's whole mindset was a photo in 2019 when she was playing for Orlando Pride. She was snapped exchanging huge smiles with a small fan, who had the same limb difference as her; the two were touching their left arms together. Pickett had avoided posting many photos of herself where her arm was visible; after the huge reaction to the elbow-bump, she began to reassess.

"I want to be an advocate for others like me, and for the longest time I didn't use my platform well enough," Pickett wrote later on her own Instagram account.

She is now one of the highest-profile female players advocating for a cause close to their hearts.

"Being a professional athlete, especially a woman, you feel like you have to just be perfect all the time, and you feel like you don't always get the respect that men get, and so every part of your life has to be perfect to get that respect," she reflected. "Especially with how much social media has taken off in the past couple of years, I remember not wanting to stand out for anything other than just being a good soccer player. All the things on social media, all the people that hide behind computers and screens – I knew that if I put my arm in a lot of photos that there would be things that were said about it that would probably hurt my feelings.

"After that photo, it switched. Of course there were definitely comments on there that were not very nice, but the pros outweigh the cons, with putting my arm on social media and celebrating who I am. I thought to myself that it was almost like I was letting the community of limb difference down, it was almost like an injustice to them: how am I going to say, 'Just be yourself and love who you are' if I wasn't even putting my arm on social media? There are so many people out there that I met through that picture going viral, that I'm like, 'I should be standing up for these people and for people like me', so that was kind of how everything turned after that picture."

One of the ways in which she took on a higher-profile role was her endorsement of a Nike boot design, the Phantom GT Flyease, with a fold-down heel enabling the foot to slide in, and a wrap-around closure rather than laces. For someone with one hand, this meant a much easier task when it came to getting ready for training or a match.

"I always say that I think it's insane that somebody [with two hands] has thought about making a boot with no laces… before someone who like me has one arm and never even thought about making a boot like that!" she grinned. "It's a really inclusive company, and I appreciate that they want to stand out and be different to other companies by helping people who don't look like the everyday athlete."

Pickett signed for Racing Louisville in 2023, moving 500 miles west from North Carolina Courage, and noticing the change in climate very quickly. She already had an idea for new gear that would work for others with limb difference.

"Gloves have definitely been an issue for me!" she said. "Putting them on is quite challenging, especially the ones that are tight at the bottom that are specific for sports... maybe I can work with [designers] and see if there's a way that we can make a glove for my arm... I think that could be something that's really cool."

Pickett's parents, Mike and Treasure, had been incredibly supportive and inspirational to their daughter. She wondered if now she could use her position as a high-profile soccer player to be a role model or inspirational figure for young people who perhaps did not have the same kind of strong, caring adults in their own lives.

"I just want to be there for somebody who maybe doesn't have the confidence to be themselves," she said, "to be there for someone who doesn't have confidence to be themselves or who doesn't want to stand out, just like me, for being different. I just want to help as many people as I can, especially, I feel, young kids, because teenage years aren't very fun when you're different. It's just the honest truth. You just want to be like everyone else.

"If I can just help one kid understand that their difference is important and it's good to be different – you don't want to be like everyone else. I never understood that until I got older, and now that I'm older, I do wish that I could just get it across to kids and to people that having an imperfection is beautiful and you don't have to hide that."

Athlete Ally's website is unequivocal about the organisation's motivations.

"Athlete Ally believes that everyone should have equal access, opportunity, and experience in sports — regardless of your sexual orientation, gender identity or gender expression. Our mission is to end the rampant homophobia and transphobia in sport and to activate the athletic community to exercise their leadership to champion LGBTQI+ equality."

Hudson Taylor founded Athlete Ally after his eye-opening experiences at college. A star at the University of Maryland, he was ranked as the second-best wrestler in the USA; he was also studying theatre as his major. Where the drama studio was welcoming and inclusive, the gym was riddled with sexism and homophobia. Taylor took the small step of wearing an LGBTQ equality sticker on his headgear – an action that garnered media attention but also inspired others around the country, who felt empowered by his show of solidarity and his action of activism. He realised that as an individual in a less celebrated college sport, he had made a genuine difference to people, and went on to set up an organisation that encompassed the allyship and advocacy of some of global sport's biggest names.

In addition to their work in education, offering training to athletes, teams and leagues, and in policy-making, from grassroots to Olympic and Paralympic standard, perhaps Athlete Ally's most famous asset was their ambassador programme. By 2023, they had more than 400 athletes, either current or retired professionals who had played their sport at the very highest levels, who wanted to use their position and their platform to promote LGBTQI+ inclusion, either as a straight ally or as members of the community themselves.

Lori Lindsey had been part of the USA team that lost in the final of the 2011 Women's World Cup. Her team-mate and close friend Megan Rapinoe had become something of a celebrity during that tournament, easily identifiable with her bleached blonde crop of hair, and impressively used as an impact sub towards the end of matches. Ahead of the 2012 Olympic Games, Rapinoe had been asked to do a magazine spread devoted to out gay athletes. Her agent asked her if she wanted to talk about her sexuality and her private life in a public domain.

"I was like, 'Yes, you do,'" said Lindsey. "I answered for her – 'Let's go! I would [do a magazine interview], but I don't have the same platform as you do right now.'

"We hadn't been living a closeted lifestyle or anything. There just wasn't a platform to be like, 'Hey, we're queer athletes and here's our story.'"

The USA team won the gold medal at the 2012 London Olympic Games, and they continued their rise to global stardom, becoming household names, regularly attracting tens of thousands of fans to their matches. Rapinoe – so easily identifiable – became even more famous, with more and more media outlets wanting to speak to her, and the rest of the squad also got their opportunities to speak about themselves, their lives and causes that mattered to them.

"I had a few publications that were like, 'Hey, you want to tell your story?', and I was like, 'Absolutely, let's do it,'" said Lindsey. "That's when Athlete Ally really started to take shape as well. I understood in a bigger capacity, partially because it was coming towards the latter part of my career as well, how important it was to use our voice with the platform that we had. I had been so fortunate with my mom who has been an out lesbian my entire life, since I was very young – the power of that and living your truth. We weren't closeted, but then to be able to be offered an opportunity to really speak about it – Athlete Ally on a much broader scale was consistently that platform.

"It was perfect timing for Athlete Ally to come in and really start to engage in women's football in particular."

Lindsey had been a big part of Athlete Ally's work in promoting trans rights, and most especially defending trans children's rights to play sport. She had spent years going into schools and talking about gay rights and LGBTQI+ inclusion; now she was writing opinion pieces for newspapers, and even testifying in Missouri's Senate.

"It's powerful and it's important work," she said, "because I know sport is a vehicle… outside of winning championships, it's competition, it's healthy, mentally, physically, and these kids, that's what they want to do. They're not trying to win a gold medal. They want to play and we're here trying to – well, not all of us, but some select few are trying to say, 'No, you can't do that,' and I find that absurdly ridiculous."

Lindsey had always loved being able to be a strong role model for children who perhaps did not have the same kind of positive adult presence in their own lives.

"In my playing career I would get letters or messages that were from younger kids, saying, 'Thank you for being a role model. It's given me strength.' You realise the power of visibility and what that means for players or just kids in general who are coming up and struggling – they may not be struggling with their sexuality [but with something else] – how much that helped. It looks really different I think from person to person depending on their journey, but that is a responsibility in some ways for me personally. Given my mom and my childhood, I felt the responsibility was to be out and display that, because I knew how powerful that was for me."

Lindsey and Rapinoe had two ironic jokes they liked to make.

"One, you can't win a championship without a gay on your team, so you might as well be out about it," laughed Lindsey, "and if we had to choose to be gay or straight, we would be gayer than we actually are. That's how we've lived. That has been our friendship. It's always been about [being] welcoming and saying it's OK, and, as cliche as it might sound, it gets better, it does. It is a matter for each individual, but when you can see it, that helps as well."

Lindsey hailed the next generation of female footballers, who spoke openly about their relationships yet only as tangential to their football, but noted that their freedom to do so had been developed by those who had gone before them.

"That's why it's so important to have the Megan Rapinoes, because it normalises it all. Now we're seeing [Arsenal duo] Beth Mead and [Vivianne] Miedema as a couple right now. We're seeing a spread with [Australia's] Sam Kerr and [the USA's] Kristie Mewis. My friends Ashlyn Harris and Ali Krieger, they have two young kids. It's changed. It's changed quite considerably: 'Actually, this can be your story.'"

Being a visible role model to illustrate possibilities and to celebrate diversity was something about which Layah Douglas also felt strongly. When she was thirteen, she played for her school team. She scored plenty of goals, but on one occasion, her strike was marked by one of the opposition making a racist remark to her.

Douglas told the referee, who failed to take any action, so instead her coach took the whole team off the pitch, and left.

"That's the one that stands out the most," she said. "We were such a young age. How would that come about? And the referee was grown, and would have known it was wrong."

By that time she was also used to sexist comments, having played with and against boys in an area where few girls took up football.

"I'd be told, 'Oh, you're good for a girl, I thought you were going to be rubbish,'" she remembered. "I was really grateful that they said that, and now when I look back, why would they even assume that?"

Of mixed Jamaican, Indian and Irish heritage and born in the United Kingdom, Douglas spent her childhood playing for

Bristol Academy (now Bristol City) as well as Gloucestershire County and the England pathway camps. After being released by City, she gave up football for a while before being encouraged back into the game by a former coach, and then signed for Bristol Rovers. In her time there, she had already been named the PFA Community Champion for two consecutive years, celebrating her outreach work, talking to young people in schools about discrimination in football.

Her first panel event was in collaboration with Show Racism the Red Card, the anti-racism organisation led by former Newcastle United goalkeeper Shaka Hislop. When she agreed to speak to a group of schoolchildren, she did not realise it would be hundreds of them from across the area.

"They asked a lot of questions!" she grinned. "But because they had done a day of workshops, they were quite education on racism and discrimination, so the questions they were asking were quite hard to answer.

"They were asking, 'When do you think racism will end?' and I was like, 'Wow. Well, I hope it will be soon.'"

Afterwards, Show Racism the Red Card invited her to become an ambassador, meaning she would be part of local workshops, speaking on panels, and creating digital content, advocating for their anti-racism work. In the year following England's win at the 2022 Women's Euros, it was a particularly opportune time; questions had been asked in many quarters about the squad's lack of players from non-white backgrounds, and it was something Douglas had noticed in her own career, even if she did not think it was deliberate. She herself had been largely inspired by her father to play football.

He had retired early from the game due to the degenerative spinal condition ankylosing spondylitis, and had encouraged his oldest child as soon as she could kick a ball. She had also looked up to the Brazilian star Ronaldinho, but other than that she was not aware of many female players at all, let alone ones from a similar background to her.

"I find in the majority of women's football, especially the teams that I've played in, it's not that multicultural," she said. "The majority of the time, I was the only player that wasn't white.

"When I was released from the [Bristol Academy] set-up, I didn't take it as a racism thing, but at the same time, I was like, 'Now the whole team are white.'" She described it as "unfortunate", wishing there was more diversity in women's football. This monoculturalism had not been the case when she played for boys' teams, and she was pleased to note the changing demographic of the Bristol Rovers team as the community trust worked to develop links across the city. Not only that, she was delighted to be able to be a visible figure for little girls to look up to, just as she had admired Eniola Aluko, Fran Kirby and Nikita Parris when she began to watch women's football herself.

"If you don't have someone that's maybe from the same background as you to look up to, it can be hard to be inspired to actually play. That might be why there [are fewer] people that aren't white in female football – because you haven't got as many role models."

HIGHS

A thirty-match unbeaten streak is something to treasure. When Sarina Wiegman's proud record as England coach came to an end in April 2023, less than 100 days before the start of a Women's World Cup they had been heavily tipped to win, outsiders might have been surprised by how pragmatic she was about it. The Lionesses had not lost since 2021, and as well as winning the Euros they had also won the inaugural Finalissima against CONCACAF champions Brazil. Wiegman did not see a single defeat as a problem; it was an opportunity to learn.

"I'm not worried. I don't worry very quickly," she told the media.

"We know we have to be at our top level and that's when we go into the World Cup too.

"Every game we get some warnings – against Brazil we got some warnings in the Finalissima. We know where we want to go to and what we have to do. I don't think we're losing momentum, I think it's building."

Those who have achieved great success simply have a different and thrilling mindset that contrasts starkly with the rest of the world. Once they have achieved their initial aims, they do not rest on their laurels; they set new targets, discover new ambitions, and go out to conquer their challenges once more.

Four Women's Champions League titles, five league crowns across two of Europe's top competitions, plus various domestic cup wins – that would not be a bad tally for any footballer. Add to that an Olympic gold medal and a European Championship win with her nation, and anyone would forgive Josephine Henning for revelling in her success.

"I can't even tell you where my Olympic medal is right now," she admitted. "I know that the FIFA Museum [in Zurich] had it but at some point I have to check. I have no clue where my Champions League medals are."

The former Germany international spent time at some of Europe's leading clubs – Turbine Potsdam and Wolfsburg in her home country, Paris Saint-Germain and Olympique Lyonnais in France, and two spells with Arsenal in England. Her career could, however, have been very different had she followed one of her other passions. Indeed, when she finished her compulsory schooling, she hoped she might be able to combine two of her loves, playing professional football while studying at art school. She signed up for the art course in Potsdam before her then-coach Bernd Schroeder ("A legend, but he's like military school," she described) told her it would not be feasible as she would be training two or three times a day.

"I was like, 'No, not possible, I have to be there at the university'," she recalled, but Schroeder's insistence won out. "My master plan didn't really turn out [the way I had intended], but I managed to do an internship in a graphic design company. It was not a decision, like, 'OK, no, [I choose] football, and art is gone.'"

Henning's earliest memory of football was playing with her father and brother in a public space. Her father had been a decent player himself, but he had not been able to turn professional, and when he saw his daughter demonstrate some talent, he sought out a girls' team for her, meaning that unlike many of her friends she was in an all-female set-up from the start.

"For me, now, I can say he was like the biggest feminist," said Henning. Her father had become an actor, her mother was a theatre designer, and they lived together in what she described as a "happy, hippy family" until her parents separated. "I never felt like I had any problems. It was just exploring things with him. So he was always like, 'Hey, I couldn't – I was not allowed to do this. You can try, here you go.' So I feel like I profited from a [previous] generation, from his traumas.

"Maybe there was a push because he couldn't [play football professionally]. But I think you don't live your dad's life… I still feel like I made my own path."

The girls' team her father found for her included players who were perhaps not as good as her, but she made friends and loved the sport immediately, describing it as an addiction.

"I realised that I was a little bit quicker, I was physically a little bit better," she said, attributing it to her evenings and weekends playing football in the community ball cages. "I was like, 'OK, this is not challenging', and then I just kept playing because it was fun: I felt like, 'OK, I'm a little bit faster and I always get the ball' so it was just fun! I think that's what kept with me."

That first club was not a big set-up, and they did not have much money, but they ran holiday camps to encourage more girls into the sport, not necessarily to create top professional players, but to give girls that sense of fun and friendship.

"There was so much love in there," said Henning. "You can see it's not [all] about football."

After her parents split up, Henning's father suggested she look for a team that played at a higher level. The fifteen-year-old Henning tried out one club, but did not enjoy their training sessions, which focused more on fitness and running than anything else. Her father was also unimpressed by their coach, who suggested that the teenage Henning lose some weight ("I was really skinny!" she remembered). The second club she tried was much more what she wanted: "a big friendly bunch of friends from the first moment on, so I was like, 'Oh, I think that's where I'll go.' So I never decided for the football, [the intent of playing] professional football. I just said, 'Oh, that feels better.'"

For such a decorated footballer, Henning's narration of her career was fascinating in how she emphasised the importance of fun. She did not seriously consider how she could make it her career until she finished her schooling with the Saarbrücken academy at the age of eighteen. She had received international honours at junior age-group level, and knew that if she wanted to be a senior international, she would need to turn professional and move to a bigger, top-flight club. That was when she came up with her ultimately thwarted scheme to attend art school and play professional football simultaneously. Having realised that she had to concentrate on football – and almost as if the decision between her two potential career paths had been made for her without her noticing – she packed up her art materials and put them away.

"I put it in a box and said, 'No, I have to focus now,'" she said. It caused her a great deal of anguish, and eventually she decided she needed to start creating art again.

"I can tell you I needed it. It was just an inner motivation. I drew something, just a paper and pencil, or on the plane I was always sketching, or in a hotel room; you can't bring all the paint but you can sketch, so it was always there."

It made her feel better, but the more she did it, the more she realised that it was an indicator that something was missing in her life.

"I feel like if you have that creative inner motivation to do something, you miss something, or you miss expression, you miss all these things, and sometimes it's good to listen a little bit more. Sometimes I paint and I don't even know what I paint and then I step back and look at it and I was like, 'Oh yeah, right. Come on. You're painting like half of your family, you miss your family,' something like that."

Henning described this "unboxing" process as "a little fight", because she knew that if she took up her art seriously again, it would unlock something within her and it would mean a major life change – she would retire from football. During her time with Lyon and her last spell with Arsenal from 2017, she found herself buying huge canvases to work on. This was, she was sure, an indicator that she was about to experience a big change in her life. She had suffered a knee injury and could potentially return to elite football, but her time away from the pitch gave her perhaps more time to think.

"That was the moment where in my inside, I knew, 'OK, I think it's going to turn now,' but very, very fun, and very scary because the second you know: 'OK, you always had that second passion. You want it to do it. So it's going to turn now. Oh, my God!' It wasn't like, 'Phew. Come on. Let's end it.'"

One of Henning's fears was her non-traditional route into art and whether she was fully prepared for her new job. She had not been able to study her craft; all her peers would have graduated university and begun to settle into their own style.

"By now we're thirty. They went through all the highs and lows, and I was playing football. So I knew I actually I had to fight with myself: 'No, don't listen to all the many little voices that tell you it's going to be hard and how are you going to handle it.'"

The more she considered it, the more she realised her second career in art was grounded in her first career in football. Everything she had learned in her life up until that point – whether it was winning the Champions League or recovering from serious injury – had given her the tools she would require to become an artist.

"The way I learn is I go and do it, and then I crash, or I succeed and then I do it again. So I would never think too much about starting.

"If you want to learn something different, and you want to get better, you have to overtrain, not too much, but you have to do something you've never done before. So you have to overtrain, and then it becomes normal and relaxed when you do it a little bit. If [as a footballer] you want to connect to synapses in your head for a new thing, you do it in the week, over and over, way too much, and then you have one situation in the game, like ninety minutes on Sunday, you do it automatically, like unconscious, and that's I think how I learned."

Perhaps, she thought now, art school would not have been the right route for her anyway.

"I don't regret it, because I learned so many over-stimulations from life, because what I did with football was way over the top: what you train, what you do, the people, and so many topics... all the extremes in football in ten years or fifteen years [of a professional football career], so I maybe didn't learn a lot about [art] technique but I learned a lot about life."

Henning had enjoyed playing football, but collecting medals and trophies had never been the motivator for her. She looked back on her professional career with fondness for how she had progressed as a person and the opportunities football had presented to her, but was always keen to reiterate that success as a footballer did not necessarily make anyone a better, wiser, or stronger person than someone who had not gathered sporting garlands for their entire lives. Indeed, she felt strongly that the value others placed on footballing achievements was simply wrong.

"Our society works in a very sad, weird way. I'm happy I have all the trophies because now that allows me... to talk to so many different [people] and get invitations and I can learn from this. The biggest thing I love is to learn.

"I'm not about the titles, but it allows you so many things and people talk different[ly], they see you different[ly]. It's sick, it's actually sick, but this is how our society and how our brains work, sadly, but for me, [winning was about learning] so many things through football."

She gave the examples of learning about how a person's desperation to win could change them for the worse, or how a weaker team could win against a technically superior team, or how people in different countries had different cultural expectations.

"The English people are super different to the French and to the Germans, and I know that that's something I learned," she said. "I learned a lot about me, how people see me, so as a German I'm super direct. People [in England] think you're nosy from the first second, but for me, I haven't even started! I was very friendly. I learned so many things where you profit in your second life."

At Arsenal, a psychology test had suggested to her that she was a natural introvert who had learnt to become an extrovert; she recharged her batteries when she was alone, but she enjoyed getting to know people and socialising with them. Needing some time in solitude made her unusual in many football club settings, she had found.

"I always need the balance between the two, so in England, if you're not in the group, or if you don't have your little group and you're on your own, you're the weirdo, and I think that makes it a little bit harder."

She had shared a house with team-mate Alex Scott, who was a similar age to her, and she liked spending time with the other players, but carved out time alone by starting her art again.

"You're 24/7 with so many people, and I think that's exactly why I started painting because it was just too much for an introvert, for someone who takes energy from being alone – but you love it, so you do it."

Henning loved her time in England mostly because she loved the city of London, but she did not like the attitude she encountered of needing to work harder and harder in order to deserve success. France's more laidback demeanour was much more her speed.

"I just love the attitude of not giving too much energy to your job, to your work: you have a social life, it's life, come on, live! They manage to do this so perfect[ly]."

Her homeland of Germany's attitude towards hard work and success was, however, even more extreme, she thought. The celebrations she had seen in England after the Lionesses won the Euros in 2022 would never happen there: "We would never celebrate a star."

She explained, "We always say: 'What did she really do? What did she win, is she really that good?'

"We don't really love stars. We don't."

That might go some way to explaining the way that Henning – with that immense, intense honours list – was now happily working in her studio as a full-time artist. Her time away from the game with her knee injury had given her some perspective – both as she now understood herself as an introvert, but as someone who had spent her whole life in football and had found herself estranged from it.

"We don't even think about the social part of being injured. Not at all. In any country.

"No one is giving attention to the social part when you're away from the group.

"You are so alone from the first second you're injured with an ACL or something like that. We don't integrate that at all. No team, no club. I haven't seen that, which is a shame, but actually it's honest because football, if you're good, you're a star – in any sport – and if you're bad, you know you are gone."

Henning's words reflected those of Tammy Waine – a player ten years her senior. She said that only when a footballer had retired could she be honest about the problems and struggles she faced during her career, particularly during injury: "If they play, they still have to be strong." Henning had joined up with her friend and fellow international Tabea Kemme to create a company called Sports for Education, intended to help institutions understand their players on a deeper, more holistic level. They argued that it was not more expensive to create individualised plans for everyone; it was simply a different system that required a different way of thinking and adjusted investment. Henning had come to the conclusion that far from football reflecting society, as she had initially thought, society actually reflected football.

"Because football is such a big escape for everyone in the world, maybe it has to be the other way: that whatever we do in football can reflect and can be integrated in society. Imagine what kind of power football has. Yeah, I actually I think it goes this way."

Henning also sat on the board of a foundation founded by the German federation, which was working to combine art and football ahead of the next European Championships. It was her first step back into the sport after her retirement.

"When I stopped, I was like, 'OK, I need football.' But first of all, I had to get away. I couldn't watch a game. I didn't do anything that has to do with football, but I think that's natural and I think you need to heal, to get away, and then you come back if you really love it."

The art foundation was her comeback, which she described as a "perfect" chance to combine her loves. She also worked in the media as a co-commentator for some high-profile matches, and she thought she got those offers due to the medals she had won as a player.

"To be honest, this is where my name is always up in the front, and then opens the doors," she said. She loved giving her opinions on matches, but veered away from describing herself as an expert or a success, even in sporting terms, opting instead to narrate her life at the moment almost through a prism of philanthropy, being able to give back something to football through her work, and to the world through her expression in her art.

"I don't even know what success means, but for me, success, it would be when people see my art. I think that would be the success. For now, I'm very happy with all my little fights: how to understand life, and understand how and where I want to go, and how to be an artist."

"I never even thought I'd go pro."

Gina Lewandowski was one of the most successful American players of her generation when it came to domestic trophies, with one UEFA Women's Cup (now Champions League), two German Cups, and three Bundesliga titles to her credit. She had picked up numerous accolades while at college, so one might have expected her to step right up to professional football. The problem was that the USA had no professional women's league when she graduated in 2007. The Women's United Soccer Association had folded in 2003, and its replacement, Women's Professional Soccer, did not launch until 2009. There was no obvious route for her to continue her stellar career and make a living from it.

Lewandowski had begun playing as a small child, kicking a ball around with her neighbours and her friends in school, but it was not just football that she loved. She competed in softball, volleyball, cross-country and more, specialising in soccer and basketball when she got to high school.

"I think they're very translatable skills between the two, with the side shuffling, the jumping, the boxing out," she reflected, "and I think me playing basketball really helped me be successful in soccer and vice versa." She loved the community and friendship she found in sport, and continued playing at school and at local clubs rather than at an elite club further afield; in a single-parent household there were limited resources. However, Lewandowski's talent caught the eye, and unusually she was scouted by a college directly from her high-school team. She was offered a place at Lehigh University, which met her criteria of a Patriot League school, one step below Ivy League, which would afford her a good education as well as great soccer experience during her four years there. The campus was about fifteen minutes from her childhood home, meaning she was familiar with the area but got to know a different part of the city. She studied a bachelor's degree in biology all day, and trained in the evening, playing a game once or twice a week, but ultimately intending to go into graduate school to specialise in physical therapy or nutrition.

In her senior year of college, Lewandowski realised that playing football professionally could be an option. Without a domestic league to watch, she had few role models showing her that it could be done, although she had been to a handful of US national team matches when they were hosted at Lehigh. Then she visited her aunt in Frankfurt during her winter break from college, and after discussions with her family, friends and coaches, she saw that playing in Germany would give her the chance of being paid for what she loved to do.

"My best friend was like, 'Why don't you play in Germany? You have relatives here, you have contacts,' and I was like, 'Actually, maybe! Maybe! Let me try it.'"

When Lewandowski got back to the USA, she began to make contact with agents and clubs, setting up trials with clubs in Germany, and returned to Europe in the summer of 2007.

"Frankfurt at first said no!" she laughed, referring to the club that eventually gave her her first professional contract. "They're like, 'We don't need you. We don't want you. We don't know who you are.'"

She then went to rivals Duisburg to train with them for a week, and the response there was much more positive.

"They said, 'Yeah, you're good. You're not fit' – because actually I tore some ligaments in my ankle back in the fall and I really wasn't fit but I have a soccer IQ – and they said, 'OK, well, you have the IQ, you look like you know the game, but you're just not fit.' They wanted me to lose three kilos. They wanted me to work on my fitness."

Lewandowski was prepared to do that, but her family in Germany really wanted her to stay closer to them than a two-hour journey, so she went back to Frankfurt and told them that she had another club interested in signing her. She might have exaggerated Duisburg's interest slightly, but she wanted to get more than a week's trial at Frankfurt to prove what she could do. They gave her a month and it sealed the deal.

"Within that month, I progressed – the language, the mentality, the style of play. I got more comfortable and I ended up earning a spot right away and started in the first game, started the whole year, and won the Champions League, or the UEFA Women's Cup, with them right away."

Lewandowski was a rarity in the Frauen-Bundesliga as most teams relied heavily on home-grown German players.

"Frankfurt in the beginning was like, 'We don't really like to do foreigners because they don't really acclimate well, don't really speak the language, and their style.' I was like, 'Come on, give me a chance! I'm not [just] any American, I'm not any foreigner!' and I think they were pleasantly surprised at how well I integrated myself."

Of course, she was able to settle in well with the support of her family, and she had accommodation and a car, so the club did not have to make any arrangements for her. Lewandowski's swift success led to a handful of other Americans following in her footsteps, with Ali Krieger, later a multiple World Cup winner, joining her at Frankfurt.

"It was cool to be that little trailblazer," she said. "We saw a lot of US national team players come over later on, and I think they just started to see just how much of an amazing opportunity [it was] to play overseas – the quality, the style is different."

Her second contract with Frankfurt ran out in 2011, a World Cup year, meaning the German domestic season concluded early, in April, to allow international teams time to prepare. With Women's Professional Soccer now established as a professional league in the USA, Lewandowski thought it might be a good time to return home, and signed for Western New York Flash.

She chose her words carefully when considering her time there; although she had wanted to wait for WPS to stabilise after its launch in 2007, by 2012 it had in fact folded, and she was playing there during its final months.

"It was a little bit of an adjustment," she admitted, grasping for the right words to describe the shock she felt and the stark contrast between Germany and the USA when it came to top-flight women's football. "Coming back to the states, it took me a while to adjust to the US mentality... I really enjoyed it. It was a great opportunity just to get back into the American culture and soccer environment."

The level of organisation and professionalism off the field was not as high as she had been used to in Frankfurt, and she knew she would be heading back to Germany.

"I was grateful for playing overseas because I don't think I would have been happy in the States, playing there, and I didn't see the benefits of playing in the States, because the organisation wasn't there, the financial stability wasn't there, the benefits all year round weren't there. Germany, you had that security all year, you have that twelve-month contract, so a stable income, medical benefits, you got to play all year round. So it was for me more advantageous to play in Germany."

She spent one more year with Frankfurt before signing for Bayern Munich in 2012. Bayern had not yet then embarked on their journey to become one of the giants of the women's game in Europe, although their men's side most certainly had; in the 2012/13 season they would win the UEFA Champions League for the first time in over a decade. Lewandowski anticipated an exciting challenge to help the Bayern women raise their game.

"I went to Munich and was seen as more of a leader, someone who could really come in and stabilise their backline as a centre back, take on more of a leadership role because of the younger players," she explained. "It was the first time living on my own, I got to speak a lot more of the language because I was integrated more into the social aspect because I was living close to [the other players], whereas in Frankfurt I was living with my family away from everybody. So I really had got to dive into the team, the culture, the language and actually playing for Bayern Munich.

"The men's side is just a phenomenal club at the level they're at and we had a lot of perks there with them: being able to go to their games and eat lunch at the facility, watch their trainings.

"It was definitely an opportunity where I was just excited to grow and have a new change of scenery and it was definitely a great environment."

Lewandowski helped Bayern to two league titles, in 2014/15 and 2015/16, and had been intending to stay there for several more years. She signed a contract extension and had been considering a role there after she concluded her playing career, but on a visit back to the USA in 2018 she noticed that her father and stepfather were both suffering declining health. Bayern agreed to allow her out of her contract, and she returned home in 2019. Unsurprisingly, NWSL clubs were interested to find out that Lewandowski was back and available, and Sky Blue – based in Jersey, just over an hour's drive from each of her parents – were the ones to secure her signature. They also supported her as she started to prepare for her life post-retirement.

"When I was in Germany, one of the benefits of me signing one of my contracts – the last contract – was getting my coaching license. That was one of the perks, because I knew I wanted to eventually coach, and so they helped me get my UEFA B licence. Growing up, I always had a passion to give back to the next generation. I've worked with local camps here [in my home area], organisations for youth, working summer camps when I was in high school, and when I got to college, I worked in college camps in the summer. I didn't really know to what capacity, what level coaching I wanted to do, but I knew I wanted to do some sort of coaching or mentoring or giving back, and then when I got to Sky Blue, the NWSL Players Association ended up subsidising the coaching license here in the States, so I took on that opportunity to be able to add to my resume, grow on the side, and really just create more of a coaching education alongside of my playing career."

Lewandowski's life had come full circle. At the start of 2023 she was appointed assistant coach for Lehigh University's women's soccer program. The office and the pitches were just the same as she remembered, but she was now planning to use her experience and her success to support today's college women towards greater things.

"It's just really cool being able to take the knowledge that I've received throughout my career and bring it back to Lehigh and really help this next generation. The head coach [Lauren Calabrese], she was the assistant coach the last six years and I actually played with her at Lehigh – she's been there for such a long time to have seen the program grow. We've been really trying to develop the program, develop the individuals, and create more of a holistic approach to sports development and sports performance and create a better student-athlete experience for the girls."

That meant using other resources, such as sports psychology and nutrition, and it was very different to Lewandowski's own college experience, which focused just on "soccer and school", as she put it.

"I truly believe we're holistic beings. We're not just physical beings. We're mental, emotional, spiritual, intellectual, and when you nurture every aspect of your being, then that's when you can be the best version of yourself.

"There's a lot of pressure and expectations, especially at the college level now more than ever, there's more stress, more busyness than ever, and it's just – 'how do we help these young women grow and become young adults and prepare them for the real world after college?'"

Having Lewandowski as a role model must surely be something the college players valued, and she worked hard to make her life lessons relevant and understandable for them.

"I think they do respect me, and they respect our head coach. I think they do see that I've lived it, I've been there. I have some great knowledge that I've collected but I also want to meet them where they're at. They are not professionals. They are still younger adults in their learning and growing, and they don't know what they don't know. They do respect me and my perspective, but I also want to hear their perspective and meet them halfway as well, and it's been fun. They're very open. They're very honest, and it's been neat because we're very real with them. I'm like, 'I made mistakes. You made mistakes. I struggle with certain things. We're all human.' I think that's the best way to coach and so you can earn that respect as well [as being] very relatable to these women."

In the early part of 2023, Lewandowski had just moved into a new home in Pennsylvania, and a lot of the memorabilia of her career was still in boxes, including her Champions League medals and shirts. She intended to have some on display eventually, but unpacking had been fairly low down her list of priorities as she embarked on a new chapter.

"I feel like I've been going non-stop and haven't really had time to unpack everything and nicely display things," she said. "I may have my jerseys over here in a frame, I want to hang them up. So these are things I want to do to showcase my career but also just be proud of where I've been and keeping perspective to that. That was many years ago. Now it's time to move on, and focus on a different passion."

To score the winning penalty in any match is thrilling. To score it in a shoot-out to win a trophy for one's country is exceptional. Swedish striker Pia Sundhage did that at the age of twenty-four, in the inaugural Women's Euros in 1984, netting the last kick in the second leg of the final to secure the triumph.

To Sundhage, England was one of the countries synonymous with football. Women's international teams so rarely had the chance to test themselves against one another; with the establishment of a European Championship, that had finally happened.

"We really wanted to know how good we are – 'how good are we?' We needed some sort of answer [to] that question and the only way to answer it is to play the best," she said. "We felt like we were unstoppable. There was a little bit [of a crowd] in Sweden, there were journalists and so on. Going to England 1-0 up, I still felt that we were unstoppable, but the press coverage, the media coverage wasn't there, to be honest. [But] as a player, you don't care. You just want to play the final."

Winning trophies was a habit for her by that point, having won leagues and cups domestically, and she went on to lift more for both Jitex BK and Hammarby, where she became player-coach. She also enjoyed more success internationally, with second- and third-place finishes at subsequent Euros, and a bronze medal at the first-ever Women's World Cup. Sweden had gone to China in 1991 knowing very little about any of the non-European countries they might play, drawn in a group against the USA, Brazil, and Japan, then the hosts in the quarter-finals – with Sundhage scoring the only goal of the game to see them through to a semi-final against near-neighbours Norway, a team they knew very well. Norway were comfortable winners, 4-1, but Sweden reclaimed some dignity with a thumping 4-0 triumph over Germany in the third-place play-off. They returned home knowing they were officially one of the very best teams in the world.

"Nobody cared," she reflected.

Women's football may have boomed in the twenty-first century, with England finally invited to play home matches at Wembley, with sell-outs there positively expected. Sundhage, however, scored a goal there for Sweden in a friendly in May 1989 as the visitors won 2-0 in front of a crowd of 3,150. It was a curtain-raiser for a Rous Cup match between the England men and Chile, which was a goalless draw played out in front of 15,628 fans.

"I remember when we walked in the locker rooms, we were not allowed to use the men's locker room, we were somewhere else," she recalled.

Sundhage was a women's football superstar, even if her achievements were not necessarily recognised more widely. Her face was on a postage stamp in Sweden in the 1980s, something of which she remained very proud. Yet her playing days are perhaps less well known than her stellar managerial career. The FIFA World Women's Coach of the Year in 2012, she led the USA to two Olympic gold medals, and when she returned home to her native Sweden, she took them to the Olympic final in 2016, with a celebratory homecoming a sharp contrast to the ambivalence Sundhage's generation had experienced in 1991.

She had never made an active decision to become a coach; she simply had so many ideas about football that she fell into it. She would grill her own coaches about their choices and their behaviour until one took her along to a coaching course to show her that it was all much more complicated than she seemed to think.

"I was hooked," she remembered. "I really liked it, I wanted to learn everything."

Sundhage progressed through her badges right up to UEFA Pro, and was adamant that she would never stop learning about coaching or about football. The US star Kristine Lilly had once told her, "Your passion for soccer is contagious," and that had been something she had taken to her heart.

"I truly believe that there is a way to improve, and it is a learning moment," she explained. As a little girl, her ambition was to become a teacher, and the principles she would have used in teaching were the ones she took into football coaching. "I like the learning moment because it's give and take. It's not that I'm standing in front of everybody, 'Now I'm going to tell you the story.' No, it's actually the opposite. It is something, communication, between the players and me, the game and me."

In 2019, she accepted the job of head coach of the Brazil women's national team, which she saw as her biggest challenge yet. She had been drawn to the position because of the country's status in men's football history – another of the great footballing nations she had admired as a child. She led them to a win in the 2022 Copa America, which gave them a place in the first-ever Women's Finalissima – once more, a major match for Sundhage against England, but this time a defeat on penalties at a packed-out Wembley.

Her personal roll of honour was so extensive, but she joked with a degree of seriousness that the achievement she was proudest of was her longevity.

"I'm still proud to be involved in the game, and also remain humble, and try to improve my coaching and learn from things," she said. "Football is so much more than gold medals. It's the way I live, the way I'm living right now, and choosing this – and I just love it."

LOWS

Being able to lose gracefully and accept failure is just as important a part of achieving success as stringing together the wins. It might be trite, but it is true – and very tricky. The stereotype of women's sport – even at the elite level – is that it is all about fun, fair play, and friendship; that it is full of the old-fashioned Corinthian spirit where simply taking part is everything. Perhaps for many female footballers through-out history, it has been, and still is. The battles women have fought over the years just to step on to the pitch mean that of course from one angle participation is a triumph in itself. Yet there is another aspect to it. No matter how much you love football, there is always a chance it will kick you in the teeth, hand you the bitterest of disappointments, and some of the most painful experiences of your life. The challenge then is using that crushing setback to make yourself more resilient and to drive yourself on to greater success, or develop yourself as a human being.

Alicia Ferguson described the 1999 Women's World Cup as "an absolute eye-opening experience". Aged seventeen, she had been called up to Greg Brown's Australia squad to compete that summer. She was the second-youngest in that squad, and one of four teenagers, alongside a trio of mid-fielders, Peita-Claire Hepperlin, Kelly Golebiowski, and Amy

Wilson, her room-mate. She had been on track for an elite
career for four years, getting a scholarship to the Queensland
Academy of Sport at the age of thirteen and going into a
full-time training programme, with gym sessions in the day
time two or three times a week, training four or five times a
week, and her school studies in between that; indeed, Brown
had been her coach at the Queensland Academy of Sport,
and had selected Ferguson as one of the first scholarship
holders when he got the national job. It was all Ferguson
had ever wanted to do. "I was living out my dreams, being
able to eat, sleep, breathe football, which was incredible at
such a young age."

Being in the Australia squad for a Women's World Cup
was, perhaps, a bit of a surprise, but Ferguson did not expect
to get any game time. She and Wilson sat together on the
substitutes' bench in the searing heat, sheltering from the sun
under towels, and enjoying the experience; they were hoping
that nobody picked up an injury, meaning they might be called
upon. As squad players, they got to witness the grand scale of
the biggest Women's World Cup thus far, with sixteen teams
(up from just twelve in 1995), and a cumulative attendance of
almost 1.2 million (not bettered until the 2015 edition of the
tournament). The matches were all organised into double-
headers, played primarily in sizeable venues usually used for
American football; these stadia came into the mix relatively
late in the planning after the success of the 1996 Atlanta
Olympic Games, when 76,489 people went to the inaugural
gold medal match for women's football. It gave the World
Cup organisers an indication of the likely popularity of the

sport, and the possible attendances their tournament could command. It was a true spectacle, and one that was, of course, hugely impressive for a teenage girl, happy just to be there.

Australia drew their first group game against Ghana and lost their second against Sweden. They were third in the Group D table before they faced Olympic silver medallists China, who had won both their previous matches and topped the group. Coach Brown called the squad into their usual meeting the day before, and announced his starting line-up. Ferguson was in it.

Brown made three changes to his previous team. Anissa Tann-Darby replaced Sarah Cooper in the back line, twenty-eight-year-old Sharon Black made way for seventeen-year-old Kelly Golebiowski, and Ferguson came in as a third striker alongside the experienced Cheryl Salisbury and Julie Murray, the team captain. She had not played a single minute of the previous two matches, and the coach had not given her any warning that she would be starting against China. She was shocked, and could not stop thinking about the prospect of playing in front of almost 30,000 people at the New York Giants Stadium.

"That night, I didn't sleep," she said. "I was pretty nervous – just everything going through my mind."

On the day of the match, it did not get easier for her.

"The occasion got the better of me," she explained. "I was overly emotional. I was getting quite emotional as we walked out. Singing the national anthem I was pretty much in tears.

"Brownie [Greg Brown] had said that we needed to impose ourselves physically on the Chinese team, because we played

China quite a bit and obviously technically and tactically they were better than us. We tended to, when they came to Australia to play us, make the pitch size as small as possible to try and contain them!"

That was what Ferguson was thinking about at kick-off – the need to impose herself physically on the opponents as quickly as possible. That was what she was trying to do in the second minute of the match, with just 94 seconds on the clock when she put a fierce challenge in on defender Bai Jie, going through the Chinese player's right leg with her left, and sending her flying into the air and clattering to the ground.

"I probably thought I was about five yards quicker than I was," admitted Ferguson, noting wryly that it was also FIFA Fair Play Day, a celebration of the purity and honour of football. She picked herself up from the challenge, and saw referee Sandra Hunt, clad in her bright yellow kit, racing over towards her, preparing to pull out a red card from her back pocket.

"I just remember her running over and going, 'You're off.' There's a photo of me looking at the red card. It took me a couple of seconds to process, and as I looked at the clock, it was a minute 34 or something like that. Then all I could think of was, 'Don't cry till you get off the pitch, just don't cry. Don't cry.' Then I cried for pretty much the rest of the game.

"I had to get escorted down the tunnel. There was a Chinese fan hanging over [the side of the tunnel], saying, 'Go home, number 13, go home!' I started throwing things, kicking things, trying to destroy whatever I could in the changing room, actually, so our sports psychologist came in just to make sure that

I wasn't going to do anything silly, which I wasn't. I was just incredibly disappointed and angry. It was really warm out there. This was one of the top teams and I let my team down because they had to go on and try and compete against them with ten players. I couldn't face them at half-time."

The temper and distress Ferguson had unleashed in the dressing room after the sending-off was, she felt, inevitable; she did not think that any chats or support from anyone – player, coach or psychologist – would have helped her into a calmer mindset ahead of the match.

"Like any international player will say, wearing your national colours and singing the national anthem is such a proud moment," she said. "You sacrifice so much in your life. You sacrifice friendships, you sacrifice time away from family. You sacrifice so much. So when these moments come, all you want to do is do everyone proud [to whom] you had to say, 'No, I can't make that', 'I can't make your birthday', 'I can't make your wedding', whatever. That internal pressure – I think a lot of players do have it, and I just hadn't had the practice of having it consistently over and over again."

Ferguson's tale of her teenage woe was well told by now, and she even smiled as she acknowledged it was a world record – the fastest-ever sending-off at the Women's World Cup. Indeed, it was the first of her two world records, as she had been part of the Equal Playing Field longest-ever football match in Lyon. It was not only for that reason that she now thought her red card had ultimately benefited her.

"That just allowed me to take the emotion out of football, to not get too far ahead of myself, because I was too focused on the outcome rather than the process," she said. "I think at that young age, it was a pretty harsh lesson but you know what? I'm really, really glad that it happened to me that young because straightaway, I just went, 'Right, it's just another game of football, you need to focus on your first touch' or 'What's a good pass – where you're going to keep possession' rather than thinking, 'Right, I'm going to score a goal, we're going to win, I'm going to do this' – all that kind of stuff. So it really helped me focus. I enjoy football a lot more when I'm not thinking about it too much, if that makes sense: just enjoying, just being present in the moment, not over-analysing stuff."

That improvement in her mental approach, she thought, prolonged her career, and made her a better player. The following year she was part of the squad for the Sydney Olympics – a home Games for the Australia team. The Olympics are always a big deal for female footballers, with the competition much more prestigious than its male counterpart. Ferguson – still in her teens in the year 2000, of course – did not find herself as keyed up for the big occasion this time round. She was there as a bench player once again, playing back-up to the established Julie Murray and Linda "Sunni" Hughes.

"They were my idols," said Ferguson. "They were so generous to me as another forward, and so supportive, and just so helpful. Julie, in the first game, against Germany in Canberra, strained her hamstring, so I came on; again, that was the main reason why I got playing time at the Olympics. I literally remember just coming out like every game: 'All right, it's just another football match.'

"Probably the most emotional I got during the Olympics was in the opening ceremony, walking out and just 100,000 people: there was an infinite amount of camera flashes going off and the noise was so deafening when we came out. It still gives me goosebumps. Then seeing [runner] Cathy Freeman light the cauldron, and [retired four-time Olympic champion] Betty Cuthbert – that was my most emotional moment of the Olympics. The Games itself, I was back to 'we're just playing football', and that was because of 1999. That was because of getting sent off. Genuinely it was, so I'm very, very grateful for that, because I think I enjoyed that experience [of playing at an Olympic Games] and took all the pressure off me, and took all the pressure of any personal expectation.

"'Just go and enjoy it. It's just a football match.'"

"That was my biggest moment..." said Lucy Ward, "and it was the worst day of my life, football-wise."

Ward had been a familiar voice on UK football broadcasts since 2007, when she joined the BBC's coverage team for the Women's World Cup in China. In the time since, she had commentated on men's and women's football, from domestic matches to Champions Leagues to more World Cups. She was perhaps well known by the wider football-following public for her court case against her former employer Leeds United, where she had worked in the men's club's education department, first as a teacher, and then as its head. Those who had followed women's football around the turn of the millennium, though, would have known her as a player, primarily for Leeds United Ladies; although they shared a name, they were only loosely connected with the men's club.

On 1st May 2006, thirty-two-year-old Ward was part of the Leeds team that faced Arsenal Ladies in the FA Cup final. Vic Akers's Gunners were in their seventh final, and had won in all six of their previous appearances. Leeds were clear underdogs, but they were excited for the opportunity to play at a big stadium – Millwall's New Den – and for the occasion to be televised. Ward, usually a forward, was playing at centre back.

"In hindsight, which is a wonderful thing when you're older, I was quite stubborn as a player," said Ward. "I would fight everybody's battles for them, which I didn't really need to do, but I always felt like if somebody wasn't being treated right, it was always me – some others just get on with it. I always got involved in things that I probably shouldn't have done, but all of it came from a good place."

Ward was a fine player technically, perhaps one of the reasons it was she who got switched to defence; there was also another player in competition with her for one of the spots up front. Moving Ward to centre back opened up that place.

"That annoyed me as well – all that sort of rubbish that you get involved with as a younger person!" Ward added.

Nevertheless, she took her place in the back line, and within the first four minutes, she hit the lowest point of her football career.

"I gave the corner away," she recalled. "I don't know how I did it, but I got a touch on it, and it bounced past the post, as if it was just going to go straight in and I thought, 'Oh,

God.' It came over; now, I was really strong in the air, and whichever, whether it was attacking or defending corners, I usually got first contact, because I was the tallest. I attacked the ball, and actually what I should have done was just send it over because I knew that [Arsenal forward] Julie Fleeting was behind me, and as it was coming over, I was thinking, 'I'll just clear it.'

"And I literally just went to clear it, and realised that, as I turned, the goal seemed to be the biggest thing ever. It just went past the goalkeeper, and I was just like, 'Oh, God, what?' and really, it wasn't like I thought, 'Oh, I've hit it!' I thought that I was clearing it. That's what it felt like, and obviously it went off the other side," she gestured to the side of her head, "which I've never had – I've never done it before and I've never done it since, and what I should have done is just let it hit the top of my head, to go over the top of Julie Fleeting, and then go behind. Nobody would have got to it.

"I had the sense that everybody knew it was me. It was on telly, my face was on the big screen and I'll tell you what, I really argued with myself for the next thirty seconds that I was just going to walk off, I really did."

Afterwards, people told her that they had not realised it was an own goal, and that they thought Fleeting had indeed got the definitive touch; it was only after watching several replays that they realised it had come off Ward's head. It was too late by then. Ward and Leeds were thumped 5-0. She had not been able to gather herself after that mistake.

"I just deflated, and I made a mistake for the second goal, and also I'm playing out of position," she said. "I played in the League Cup final, and we were losing, and I was a little bit deflated because I wasn't playing well, [but] because I'm playing up front you get away with it, but I didn't get away with it then. It was ridiculous. I can still see it all now."

What made that day worse, though, was the hindsight that she found useful when analysing herself as a younger woman.

"It didn't get any better than that," she explained. "I didn't have another day where it was like, 'Well, actually, I'm glad I survived that day.' In other aspects of my career, I'm very lucky and I have a good job, but in football I never had that day that cancelled that FA Cup final day out. To be honest, I couldn't talk about it."

Ward feared having to go back to work the next day. In a training ground environment, she was expecting intense and incessant ribbing. Instead, she found empathy and sympathy from footballers of all levels of experience who had their own stories of a disastrous day on the pitch.

"I was thinking, 'I don't think I can do it, I can't laugh about it, because I've been battered and I've scored an own goal in an FA Cup Final and I'll probably never play in another one again,' and they were all really kind because they knew what it meant to me. But even I reckon it took nearly two years for me to even smile about it, the fact that it happened. I was absolutely devastated."

Ward had grown up always being one of the best players, wherever she was playing – whether that was school or in a training camp, her club or her country; indeed, she captained England under-21s at the age of sixteen.

"The reason I played was because I had an older brother, who's two years older than me, and the house that we lived in – that was opposite our primary school – had a big garden, so really good to play football in. When you're a second child, I don't know whether it's scientifically proved, but you've always got that sort of aspiration – and I think that I was quite tough, maybe because of having an older brother – that I just always wanted to be better than him. It might have something to do with being an Aries, I'm not sure!"

Ward's teachers at primary school encouraged her to play football; there were two girls in the year above her who also played, which helped.

"I don't ever remember thinking that I was weird until I was playing and was quite good at it – and then people thought I was weird and I wasn't bothered!" she said, estimating that she was about seven years old when she realised she was a talented player. "I never remember being put off playing by my parents, which was obviously brilliant, or by my teachers who would have been the coaches of the school team. By the time people thought I was weird, I was actually quite happy because I got loads of attention for it, and I was quite good at it; so I didn't get the weird looks until I was comfortable in the fact that I was quite good at football, and then I didn't care. That's obviously credit to my mum and dad, really."

She paused, and grinned.

"And my brother. He hated it, he stopped playing when he was in his mid-teens because I was better than him."

The rules for children's football at the time meant that girls were stopped from playing alongside boys at the age of

eleven, so Ward had to look elsewhere for a team. She spotted an advert in on the school notice board for girls' football
training in Guiseley, the other side of Leeds. She missed the
first session due to a problem with her mum's car, and the
week afterwards, her mum was told that she would struggle
having missed the first session. After much pleading, Ward
was allowed to attend, and she shone, with several years of
experience playing alongside boys. A coach asked Ward's
parents if she was interested in joining a women's team. She
was, of course, but she was not yet twelve. Nevertheless, she
joined the team, the youngest by around seven years, and was
put on the wing.

"I used to get winded regularly, because I used to run
into big women," she recalled, "and it wasn't a very good
standard, but the girls... if it wasn't for them, I wouldn't
have continued to play. They were just brilliant, and I'm still
friends with them all now."

Ward thought that when she was in her twenties, she would
have been much less accommodating of a much younger
team-mate than those Leeds players were. They would pick
her up on a matchday and drop her home again, and they
would keep an eye on her throughout.

"These were women in their early twenties, who were obviously going out drinking, they used to try not to swear in
front of me, we'd break down on the A1, and they would be
like, 'Get Lucy in the car, don't let her out!'" she laughed. "It
is only when I look back and I think, 'God, I wouldn't have
done that with a kid, when I was in my early twenties, when
I was playing football – pick them up and look after them

and take them home out of the way!' Honestly, they were unbelievable. But that's what I did for years, and I moved local clubs with them."

Ward's first years with Leeds United Ladies were as a grass-roots community club, and eventually they rose to become one of the best teams in the country, promoted to the Women's Premier League in 2001. It was still, of course, resolutely amateur, but it fitted well with Ward's commitments to school, then university, then work, allowing her to balance it with playing volleyball, which she took up as a teenager, and she liked being able to play football alongside the friends she had made as an eleven-year-old. She had had the chance to play for other clubs – for example, Bronte LFC, another Yorkshire team, which had been established as far back as the 1960s, and who had players such as internationals Sammy Britton and Clare Taylor on their books – but she was happy to stay with the people who had made her football so much fun so far. Looking back, Ward wondered what she might have achieved in football had she trained every day, or if she had taken her fitness more seriously rather than relying on her naturally high levels of ability.

"I never really pushed myself as a player early on. I just enjoyed myself playing at a level that was probably not as high as I should have been playing, and that's the reason why it took till that time to get to play in a good team to play an FA Cup final. My mates like Becky Lonergan, Issy Pollard, they all played at a high level, because they went to play for a better team, and I didn't really want to leave my friends because I was quite loyal."

The year after the FA Cup final was Ward's big TV break-through in China with the BBC. When she came back and began the 2007/08 season with Leeds, she tore her anterior cruciate ligament. That season, Leeds made it to the FA Cup final again, but Ward was not part of the team. She knew she was not physically ready for it, and she was worried about getting injured again. Instead, she headed back to the commentary box and picked up a microphone.

"I didn't want to do my ACL again at thirty-three, because of my job working at Leeds: obviously that helped me [with the 2007 injury] because they got me in touch with a surgeon, I did all my rehab there, with the likes of [Ireland international] Jonathan Douglas and Steve Stone [the former England international], just me and them in the gym at the time that I could get in there.

"So I could have played in another FA Cup Final, but I'm glad I didn't, really." She counted off the reasons. "If I'd have had an injury – I wouldn't have been match fit. It would have probably ended up even worse than the one where I scored an own goal."

The year before the FA Cup Final, Ward had played in a testimonial match for Lucas Radebe at Elland Road, scoring one and setting up another. In retrospect, that was her best day on the pitch, but she had always hoped that the highlight of her career would come on a day when she lifted silverware.

"People say things even themselves out," she said, pointing to the length of her career, and how she had been part of the generation that followed the first-ever official England team in 1972. "I just thought, 'Surely I'm not going to go through my whole career and that be what happened to me on the biggest day that I could have possibly had in football?' but that's it. Shit happens. That's what happens."

Now enjoying her career in media, she took solace from the knowledge that she had played a part on and off the pitch in giving women's football a public profile. She had never dreamt that the game would have become so popular in England, and especially relished the new-found celebrity of the Lionesses who won UEFA Euro 2022.

"It's absolute madness," she said. "It's like you get put in a box: 'Well, I'm quite happy in this little box. It's never going to be like [it is now]. I hope it is, but…' You even get convinced yourself: not that it's rubbish, but it's never going to be where it's going to be on TV all the time. It never fails to make me smile. I'm jealous [of today's players], in a nice way, that I'd like to do that, but I'm not jealous where I'm envious. I just go, 'Do it.' I mean – blooming wonderful! They won the Euros and these girls are famous now. Honestly, I think it's amazing.

"I actually probably take more pride in the fact that I was a part of that pioneer generation than anything else, to be honest, because I think I might not have been as good as these players now. Who knows? I was a good player. It's all relative, isn't it? These girls train all the time. So I might not have had the highs of the career that I had.

"We walk the dogs over at Pontefract racecourse, and I saw a dad walking with a little girl in full [England] kit, and I actually cried because it was like, 'That's it!' These little girls do not know what it feels like for their families to say,

'Ooh, football? Well, why don't you go and do whatever? Why don't you go and do gymnastics?' They don't know any different. We're at that stage now; they can go and watch Leah Williamson and go, 'That's where I want to be. I want to look like her, I want to have my hair like her, I want to dress like her.'

"My favourite footballer [as a child] was Trevor Steven, I loved Everton, and I wouldn't have even dreamt of looking at a woman footballer [as an idol], even though I admired the likes of [Doncaster Belles and England striker] Kaz Walker. I take so much pride in being part of the pioneers; if it wasn't for us lot, these girls wouldn't be where they are. That's my link to what's happening now.

"All the way through my career it's been slow coming, but I'm glad it's where it is now."

Wales have never made it to the finals of a major international football competition. After the ostensible end of the ban preventing women from playing football, a national team sprang up in the 1970s, with limited resources, support or acknowledgement from the Welsh governing body, the FAW. They secured the coaching services of Sylvia Gore, the first woman to score an official goal for England, and someone who dedicated her life to grassroots football and improving the opportunities on offer for girls. However, where neighbours England had the volunteers of the Women's FA continuing to lobby for the women's game and organising domestic competition as well as international matches, Welsh women's football was driven primarily by its players plus a handful of supportive men.

At around the same time as the English FA finally decided to take women's football under its auspices, in 1993 the players of Cardiff City Ladies nailed down a meeting with Alun Evans, general secretary at the FAW. Laura McAllister, Michele Adams and Karen Jones asked him for his – and the FAW's – support; they asked for official endorsement for their clubs, and ultimately some recognition and structure for the Wales national team. Evans was persuaded by these three young women, and was impressed by what the women's teams had been doing with so little help.

With FAW backing, Wales were entered into the 1995 European Championship qualifiers, which began in the autumn of 1993; with so little preparation compared to their opponents, which comprised Switzerland, Croatia, and World Cup winners Germany, it was unsurprising that they finished bottom of their group with no points, losing all six of their matches, scoring only five goals and conceding 36.

Even with that official rubber-stamp, Wales did not have it easy. They were set to compete in the qualifying rounds for Euro 2005 – to be hosted in England – but they were withdrawn from the competition after the draw was made, putting them into a group with Belarus, Estonia, Israel and Kazakhstan. The FAW were concerned about the cost in financially strapped times, and even though they were fined by UEFA, reports suggested that the amount of 50,000 Swiss francs levied on them as a punishment was far less than they would have had to pay to travel to their away matches and host at home.

Sian Williams, manager of the women's team, was quoted at the time as saying, "The players find this decision devastating and I find it frustrating as we would really have fancied our chances of qualifying for the finals in England in 2005.

"If Kazakhstan and Belarus, who are third-world countries in financial terms, can afford to put a team in the European Championships, why can't Wales?

"In England, women's football is officially the biggest participation sport, ahead of netball and hockey. In Wales, the FAW Trust, responsible for bringing youngsters into football, are working hard on the female side of things.

"But what sort of message does it give out when they've got nothing to go for at the top?"

Then, a teenager called Helen Lander – born in Brent, London – was concentrating on her club football for Watford, the team she had been with since childhood. Aged twenty-one, the striker was called up to the England under-23 side, playing the last ten minutes of a Nordic Cup match against Finland to receive her first international cap. A year later, she made her senior debut for Wales against Luxembourg, qualifying via her maternal grandfather. Lander – later better known as Helen Ward following her marriage – and her association with Wales's national team was to prove an enduring one, lasting until spring 2023, when she announced her imminent retirement from all forms of football at the end of the 2022/23 season.

Despite the longevity of Ward's career, she never played a major international tournament, and yet she had come so close just a few months before she decided to hang up her boots. Wales had made it to the qualification play-offs for the 2023 Women's World Cup, winning their first-round match against Bosnia-Herzegovina on October 6th, 2022, courtesy of a fabulous volley in extra time from Jess Fishlock. Ward replaced Fishlock in the dying moments of the match as Gemma Grainger's side defended in numbers and saw out the win.

It was all down to one last match five days later – against Switzerland for a place at the Women's World Cup. Rhiannon Roberts put Wales ahead in the first half before Ramona Bachmann levelled. The Swiss piled on the pressure: Ana-Maria Crnogorčević missed a penalty, netting a rebound, but as no other player had touched the ball it was disallowed, as was another from Bachmann after a video-assistant referee (VAR) ruling of offside in the build-up. As extra-time began, and then ticked away, the lottery of a penalty shoot-out seemed inevitable. Ward was still on the bench.

"It was draining, the whole game was draining because we've gone through 120 minutes a few days before against Bosnia, and although that ended really well, all that adrenaline got us through and then to face a very good Switzerland team…" Ward gathered her thoughts. "We didn't do terribly by any means and we held our own in terms of in-possession stuff. We didn't do what we know we're capable of and we invited a lot of pressure, so that constant wave of Switzerland attacks was draining to watch. I can't imagine what it was like for the girls to actually have to defend against and for the most part they did fantastically well, but it was the VAR, a couple of goals, the penalty. And I think it was just such an emotional roller coaster that by the end of that; we were all shattered.

"I knew that there was potential that I might be sent on to take a penalty and I always thought I don't want to be that player that does that [taking the place of someone else who had played the entire match]. But in the moment that [Grainger] asked me the question, 'Will you take a penalty?' I was like, 'Absolutely I will', because I had to step up."

Ward stepped on to the pitch in the 119th minute of the match, with just seconds to go until the imminent penalty shoot-out. Less than two minutes later, in added time, Fabienne Humm tapped home at the near post to break Welsh hearts. Ward's penalty-taking skills would not be needed; Wales would be watching the World Cup from afar once more.

She described the loss as "devastating". After fifteen years of playing for Wales, and edging towards her thirty-seventh birthday, Ward could not contemplate going through another gruelling qualification campaign again. Instead, she opted to retire.

"I just got to a point [to retire] once we were knocked out of the World Cup like that. My target was to retire at the World Cup in the summer and then as soon as that didn't happen, I knew that I couldn't face going through another campaign. For me, such a massive part of my football was playing for Wales, and I can't imagine playing domestic football and not international. It was all or nothing for me. So when I made the decision I wasn't going to be able to commit to another qualifying campaign, I knew that was it.

"As much as Watford particularly means to me – it's a club that is in me, it's in my blood, it's in my heart, and it still will be, I'm still hoping to be part of Watford in one way or another – I just knew that I wasn't going to be able to play and have the motivation to do everything without having that carrot of getting into the next Wales squad and trying to compete and qualify for tournaments. It's a decision that it wasn't difficult to come to. I'm really excited about what I can potentially do next."

She added a dose of humour. "The thought of not having to do a preseason this summer is something that makes me very, very happy. I've been through enough of them. I've worked out this is my twenty-second season, so nobody needs to play any longer than that, I don't think."

Ward had told the rest of the Wales squad of her decision during the February 2023 international camp, and Grainger had promised her a proper send-off in April as the team's guest and with her family in attendance at the next match.

"She didn't have to do that," Ward pointed out. "She could quite easily say, 'Thank you, see you later, I'm going to move on.'"

Ward also appreciated the ability to make her own decision to retire, rather than being nudged into it, or forced into it by injury. She knew she would be retiring as Wales's all-time record goalscorer, with 44 goals to her credit and over a century of caps, but she played that down a little despite her pride in the achievement.

"I do put it into context of a lot of my goals came a long time ago and it's been a while since I've had that sort of goalscoring form for Wales, so I wouldn't say that it's tainted it for me, but it puts into perspective how well I did do in my early years because I now know how hard it can be to score goals at international level. Obviously pride is the overwhelming feeling; to be able to play for Wales so many times and then to hold the record of number of goals scored is pretty cool, and it's very special.

"I said to my husband that another thing that I'm proud of is that every time I've been fit, I've been picked for an international squad – not always got on the pitch, of course, [but] I've always been in the squad. I suppose it's a bit of an ego thing… I didn't want to keep going until I didn't get picked any more. I know where I'm at and I know that there's other players that are now coming through that are going to go on and be amazing for Wales. I've served my time and it's up to them to take over."

Ward's career had three notable interruptions. Like so many footballers in England, her 2019/20 season had been truncated due to the outbreak of the Covid-19 pandemic, and she had suffered from not being able to train properly or play. She thought that inconsistency of schedule had had an impact on her body, meaning that she subsequently suffered lots of relatively small but irritating injuries, notably problems with her Achilles.

Twice previously, though, she had taken time out of the game to give birth to her children, first her daughter Emily, and then later her son Charlie. That was not to say she had spent months on the sidelines; indeed, she was playing for Wales again within two months of giving birth for the second time.

As a baby, little Emily had gone on some Wales camps with her mother, with then-coach Jayne Ludlow happy to accommodate the new family however she could. Ward was quietly impressed with the progress that had been made since she had her first child, although she wondered if decision-makers in football, just as in any other sphere, might be worried about employing a woman who they expected to have children in the near future. Nonetheless, she was pleased that maternity leave was now written in as a provision in players' contracts, and hoped there would be more contractual protection for football-playing mothers in the future.

"As myself and others before have hopefully contributed to where we're at now, hopefully the experiences of the next generation will then contribute to the next big step," she said.

Ward had worked on developing her career in the media, taking a sports journalism degree via distance learning with the support of the PFA in between having her children. That had given her some experience in broadcast and commentary, and she was becoming a regular voice on several radio shows, able to dial in remotely and air her views.

"I always put playing and training first, but if there's an opportunity to go and do some comms or punditry, radio, anything like that, I jump at it," she said. "It's good experience, I get to talk about men's football, women's football and everything else."

Now she would be moving on to the next stage of her life, of course likely to contain plenty of football, but not in the same way as it had done during her playing days.

"Football is literally everything," she said. "I met my husband through football. I'd probably still be at home with my mum if it wasn't for football! It is a strange thing [knowing that retirement was imminent]. I'm quite excited about it, which I think tells me it's the right decision. It's something that I've threatened to do for probably the past five years, every season now: 'This is my last one. I'm not going to do it any more.'

"Before having Emily, I thought I'd never play after having a child."

Watford marked Ward's retirement with a permanent tribute at Vicarage Road, the club's main stadium, unveiling a mural of her in action for club and country. In her final match before hanging up her boots, she was named on the bench for the FA Women's National League play-off against Nottingham Forest. With the Hornets 1-0 up with seconds to go before their promotion to the Championship was confirmed, and wanting to ensure a cameo role for their departing heroine, Ward was standing on the sidelines in full kit, waiting for a break in play so that she could replace a team-mate on the pitch for the last few moments of her career.

The break never came. The whistle blew. Watford were promoted. Ward was still at the edge of the technical area, an unused substitute on that day, perhaps, but one of the most important figures in the club's history, and with a funny tale to tell about the day she retired from football.

RECORDS

Who has scored most goals in a single World Cup?

Who has the most caps in international football?

Men's football continues to be the default format of the sport – indeed, rarely having the descriptor "men's" attached to it in the way that women's football usually does. Women's football is still viewed as secondary.

Rebecca Sowden, a former New Zealand international, had always noticed sexism in the sport she loved. She was one of the only girls playing in a boys' team, and realised that she was treated differently from the off.

"It was just this mindset of boys first, men's first: even just stupid things like going to get changed – no changing room facility. No one's even thought about me as a girl or a woman."

When the coach asked players to pair up, she was left as the last one because the boys did not want to partner a girl. Sowden felt in retrospect it might not have been deliberate, it was simply a lack of awareness; the boys and the men had not had the same lived experience as her and they did not realise how she felt.

"They can't really fully understand or appreciate unless they're wanting to," she said. "It's this vicious cycle that perpetuates itself."

Sowden now runs a marketing and sponsorship consul-
tancy specialising in women's sport, called Team Heroine.
She had launched it during the 2019 Women's World Cup
when she noticed the mammoth global viewing figures and
the lack of engagement from brands, who were failing to
understand the opportunity they had and either ignoring the
event altogether, or simply just doing the same kind of things
as they did for their men's sport mega-events link-ups. Team
Heroine's most celebrated achievement to date is a campaign
called Correct the Internet. The idea is to improve web search
engines so that they do not default to men's sporting records
and trivia, but include women as well. Web users are asked
to send feedback via an online tool when they notice that
there is an inaccuracy in a search result, where men's sport
is prioritised over women's.

"It really is about people power and it's not the search
engines fault. They're just giving people what they think
they want. Us as people have created this inherent bias in
their search engines, but then the flip side to that is it's great
– because people caused it, people can also fix it."

The campaign had gathered plenty of media attention
worldwide but also corporate buy-in.

"Everyone we've spoken to has just been like, 'How can
we support? How can we come on board?'" They had been
gifted billboard space and television spots, and global governing bodies across sports had been in touch to find out how
they could get involved. "All of us, across the board, [are]
having the same problem around when we're searching – not
just stats, but game results, or anything to do with women's

sport. We're always getting served the men's equivalent. If you've entered a non-gendered question you should get a non-gendered response. Yes, you can use gender qualifiers in it. But if you type in, 'What's the tallest building in the world?', everyone – no matter where they are, or what sex they are or who they are or if they're a women's sports fan or not – should get the Burj Khalifa."

Sowden wondered if the inequalities and stereotypes that she saw sport steeped in were off-putting to girls, and she hoped that starting to rectify some of these problems would also encourage greater participation.

"Everything from female bodies to language in sports – batsman, chairman, whatever – to coverage, it all goes back to being created with the men's-first lens. Back in the day, it was all set up with boys and men in mind. Everything has been built around it." She pointed to the slow progress with women's fit kit and boots for women. "We're still suffering the effects of this generations-long hangover.

"We're still battling that and even though it's changing, there is progress and development, the inherent bias is so deep that even on the internet, we've built that into any new systems that come along, that runs so deep, as opposed to building a new way. It's mind-boggling that governing bodies and sports and brands and everyone haven't changed or adapted or kept pace with the introduction and growth of girls' and women's [sport]. Why is the FIFA World Cup not called 'Men's World Cup' when [it's] the Women's World Cup? Such a no-brainer. Sports bodies, unfortunately, aren't the quickest to move and update, and they love tradition."

She felt that there was still a lot of prejudice around women's sport – that men's sport is and should be the main event, with women's sport taking a secondary spot.

"Maybe [men] are strong. Maybe they are faster. Maybe they're fitter physiologically. The biggest fault is that people don't understand it doesn't necessarily make it better. So there's this wrong correlation with 'stronger and faster' means 'better', which is, of course, not the case. Take tennis, for example. People love women's tennis because the rallies are longer. With women's soccer, it's maybe a more skill-based game without the diving and the ridiculous tackles and aggression. Actually, at the end of the day, sport is just entertainment. As long as there's drama, lots of goals, a close match, everyone would rather see that than faster men playing and winning 10-0 in a boring game."

Sowden was adamant that projects like Correct the Internet had the potential to change the face of women's sport, raising awareness of women's achievements.

"Women's sport, obviously, can't follow the same path as men's sport or what's traditionally been done. We have the opportunity to fast-track and catch up that 100 years that we've lost – catch up to where we need to be, then giving sportswomen the recognition they deserve. We need to think more creatively outside the box. We need to be bigger and bolder because we've got decades to catch up on and technology and innovation is one of those ways we can help fast-track that progress. Something like Correct the Internet, it might appear one small little facet of the ecosystem, [but] it again has this flow-on effect throughout:

visibility, changing that mentality of women's sports as second-tier."

Former Arsenal coach Vic Akers once revealed that Gunners legend Thierry Henry had spoken of striker Kelly Smith as the one woman who could most definitely reach the top of the men's game.

Women's football continues to be compared to the men's game. Often, this is in the benevolent way that Smith was picked out as a player good enough to compete with men – intended as a compliment but ultimately undermining the quality of the women's game, suggesting that any female player would naturally want to play alongside and against men. The same has applied for coaches; long-serving Chelsea coach Emma Hayes, as the most high-profile female manager in England, has often been linked with managerial vacancies in the Premier League, and since the Lionesses' European Championship win and their thirty-match unbeaten streak, Sarina Wiegman has been another name thrown into speculation around managerial vacancies.

When linked with the post at AFC Wimbledon in 2021, Hayes said: "I am manager at Chelsea. I manage and represent elite and world-class players and this for me is an amazing job I've spent nine years cultivating all my energy into. I'm not looking for another job."

Although she was careful to point out that she thought the skills involved in coaching and managing male and female footballers were exactly the same, and that women should be able to coach men if they wanted, just as men coach in the women's game, Hayes was also critical of the mindset that continued to treat men's football as some kind of promotion for a woman.

"Fran Kirby, Pernille Harder, Beth England, Magda Eriksson, Millie Bright, Maren Mjelde – do you want me to keep going? These are world-class players.

"Women's football is not a step down from anything. Women's football in its own right is something to celebrate and the quality and the achievement of all the females I represent, it is an insult to them that we talk about women's football being a step down, the dedication and commitment that they have."

Hayes also had something to say when asked about Wiegman's achievements at international level, praising her: "She is an amazing manager. It's the same sport, she just manages women rather than men at an extremely high level. I think some of the opinions in and around whether women could do that job [in men's football] are absolute nonsense. Of course she could do the job."

Another way that well-meaning sexism is evident in women's football is the way that female players are described in terms of a male equivalent; when Fran Kirby – one of those Hayes highlighted as world-class – first burst on to the international scene, her England coach Mark Sampson referred to her repeatedly as "Mini Messi", likening her to the Argentina legend Lionel Messi. Rather than appreciating a female footballer for her own talents and abilities, she can only be measured in how similar her style of play is to a man's.

Where nineteenth-century literary criticism used the descriptor 'the Angel in the House' when discussing a certain archetype of female character – domestic, gentle, ladylike – twenty-first-century sports journalism's language about women's football could be categorised as a narrative about 'the Angel on the Pitch'. Women's football can, on occasion, be positively compared by these reporters to the men's game, but almost always because of the players' behaviour – they dive less, they foul less, they swear less, they waste less time, and if there is any evidence of misconduct, it is either an unintended error or something which deserves huge and maximum condemnation. Female players – even at the highest level – are expected to be accessible, signing autographs and posing for selfies with young fans, and lauded as excellent role models; male players in the elite echelons are thanked for such engagement but it is unusual.

And women are still almost expected to demonstrate their gratitude for everything they receive, no matter how little, particularly as they make inroads into the male-dominated world of football and begin to take up space and resources – space and resources that, as this book has shown, are still given to boys and men without question. This infuriating situation cannot be summarised any more forcefully than by academic Dr Ali Bowes, who described that tendency towards thankfulness as one of the most frustrating parts of working within women's football.

"Lots of female athletes feel like they can't speak out because look at where they are now and where it started – we've already come so far. [It's like] if you're just the woman that keeps moaning about stuff, they'll take it all away, or they'll say, 'Well, these women are never happy!'

"It permeates across women's sport at every level, about probably any topic, to be honest. You'll have that real juxtaposition of being like, 'Oh, thank you for letting us get this far,' and then the concern around saying, 'Ooh, we've got this far, [but] actually, we really wanted to get that little bit further.'"

Female footballers at all levels are endlessly expected to prove themselves as worthy of respect, over and over again. Just look at the never-ending discourse around the quality of female goalkeepers for a great example of this; as soon as a woman makes a mistake, she knows that it will be ammunition for that continuing line of argument, regardless of how well she might play the rest of the time. Achievements are underplayed, popularity underestimated: the best female goalkeeper in the world, Mary Earps of England, played the entire 2023 Women's World Cup knowing that her replica shirt was not available for fans to purchase. Before the tournament began, she described the decision as "hugely disappointing and very hurtful", even offering to pay for their production herself. It is difficult to imagine her male counterpart ever being in a similar situation.

Meanwhile, men are hailed and praised as 'allies' for doing the bare minimum, for recognising the existence of women's football and for acknowledging its players and fans, when true allyship would be using their platform to genuinely promote and support the game and its participants. When England reached the Women's World Cup final in August 2023, neither prime minister Rishi Sunak nor FA president Prince William were in attendance, instead sending good luck wishes. Both men invoked their daughters: the Prince of Wales was joined in his video message by Princess Charlotte, and the prime minister wrote in his letter: "For my daughters, and for every girl in this country, you have made football something for them; you have made them feel they belong on the pitch."

It came a few days after FIFA president Gianni Infantino had told women in football: "I say to all the women – and you know I have four daughters, so I have a few at home – I say to all the women that you have the power to change. Pick the right battles, pick the right fights. You have the power to change. You have the power to convince us, men, what we have to do and what we don't have to do. You do it, just do it. With me, with FIFA, you will find open doors. Just push the doors, they are open."

These powerful men, in positions of responsibility, perhaps failed to recognise that they had – and still have – an opportunity themselves to help women and women's football. They could talk about it as top-class sport and spectacle in its own right, and treat its players and their achievements just as they do their male counterparts. They could recognise that women's football is a sport that men and women of all ages can enjoy watching, not just for the sake of their daughters, but because of its own merits.

With several of the teams at the Women's World Cup in dispute with federations or coaches over resources, remuneration and training, the tournament shone a spotlight on what is still missing even at the highest level of the game.

Vivianne Miedema, the injured Netherlands striker, was a vocal observer throughout the summer, concluding in an Instagram post after Spain lifted the trophy, despite the absence of several senior players due to their conflict with the RFEF: "The World Cup almost comes with a catch-22. If the teams lacking funding and investment perform well, federations will say, 'See? We're doing fine.' If teams lose, those same federations will say, 'Why should we invest in this?'" She added in an aside evidently aimed at Infantino: "We shouldn't have to pick our battles. We absolutely shouldn't have to convince men. We deserve to be treated equal[ly]."

Yet – even in the light of the controversy surrounding the behaviour of RFEF president Luis Rubiales after the final, greeting the victorious players with kisses on the lips, which the Spanish player union later described as "unacceptable" – the Women's World Cup proved, should proof have been needed, the global popularity of the game. Over 12 million people watched the final on BBC One, making it the most-watched event of the year in the UK behind the coronation of King Charles III. Before the tournament, the fixture between hosts Australia and the Republic of Ireland had to be switched from the 42,500-capacity Allianz Stadium to the 83,500-seater Accor Stadium because of the demand for tickets. With more teams competing than ever, the cumulative ticket sales of matches were unsurprisingly bigger than at any previous tournament, as there were more matches, but the average attendance at a group stage match was also higher, up to 25,476; indeed, of the stadia that hosted group matches in France in 2019, only three of them could have accommodated a crowd of that size.

Women's football needs and deserves a recognition from all quarters of its reality – its quality, its problems, the comparative lack of research about the professional game, and its continuing obstacles. Much has been achieved, of course, but there is much more still to do to ensure that women of all ages and all standards have equivalent opportunities and rewards to their male counterparts, and to ensure that some of the increased expectations and pressures on them identified throughout this book are removed, enabling them to focus on their football, whether simply for enjoyment or as they seek to excel. This will require hard work and dedication from thousands of people around the world, but this is exactly what has kept women's football alive and brought it this far. The strength and tenacity of all involved in women's football now has a new challenge.

It's time to woman up.

ACKNOWLEDGEMENTS

A heartfelt thank you to everyone who agreed to speak to me for this book, including but not limited to:

Aaron Heifetz, Alice Kempski, Alicia Ferguson-Cook, Dr Ali Bowes, Amy McDonald, Amy Rodgers, Anette Borjesson, Annica Nasmark, Annie Ward, Carly Parry, Carson Pickett, Charly Wright, Chloe Hodgson, Chloe Hudson-Jones, Chloe Mustaki, Christina Philippou, Dr Georgie Bruinvels, Gina Lewandowski, Gwyn Roberts, Harry Cuthbert, Heather Reid, Helen Ward, Helena Andersson, Isabel Martin, Dr Jacky Forsyth, Jamie Rita, Jenny Sugarman, Jess Fassnidge, Professor Joanna Wakefield-Scurr, Josephine Henning, Juan Carlos Amoros, Karen Farley, Kate Gill, Katie Chapman, Laura McWilliams, Laura Youngson, Layah Douglas, Leanne Duffy, Lisa Owen, Lori Lindsey, Professor Lucy Spowart, Lucy Ward, Mark Fraser, Nicole Allison, Pia Sundhage, Rebecca Sowden, Sal Shipard, Scott Snyder, Stephanie Rudnick, Steve Wilkinson, Suzie Betts, Tammy Waine, Will Jones, Yuki Nagasato, and Yvonne Lara.

Thank you to Julia Belas Trindade from the University of Bristol for help accessing resources. Thanks also to the plethora of agents and press officers who have put me in touch with the right people, and another special thank you to Karen Farley for all her help and advice.

Thank you to all at Hero: to my editor Christian Müller, and to Lucy Chamberlain and the team for such great publicity. It feels very fancy to write this next sentence – thank you to my agent Melanie Michael-Greer for her advice, guidance, and hilarious WhatsApp voicenotes.

Thank you to all my friends at Aberystwyth Town Women's FC, to whom this book is dedicated – I appreciate your readiness to bounce ideas around with me and your endlessly frank feedback on some of the topics I cover here. Thanks especially to Amy Jenkins, for always being so willing to talk all things ACL, and to Ffiona Evans, for her help with the accuracy of the physiology and anatomical sections – all errors remaining are purely my own. A huge thank you to Shauna Chambers for allowing me to access her incredible network of contacts across the UK, and thanks also to Lucie Gwilt and Kelly Thomas for their support.

And thank you as always to my husband Julian for the cups of tea and the biscuits, being a sounding board, for doing so many of the household chores, for resisting the urge to interrupt my Zoom calls with your comedy and your choreography, and for everything else.

REFERENCES

Cox, David, 'Does childbirth improve athletic ability?', November 4, 2014 www.theguardian.com/lifeandstyle/the-running-blog/2014/nov/04/does-childbirth-improve-athletic-ability

Criado Perez, Caroline, *Invisible Women*, 2019, Chatto and Windus

Culvin, Alex and Bowes, Ali, 'The Incompatibility of Motherhood and Professional Women's Football in England', *Frontiers in Sport and Active Living*, September 30, 2021 www.frontiersin.org/articles/10.3389/fspor.2021.730151/full

ESPN.co.uk, 'Chelsea boss Emma Hayes: England's Sarina Wiegman could manage in men's football', August 2, 2022, www.espn.co.uk/football/uefa-womens-european-championship/story/4711457/chelsea-boss-emma-hayes-england-sarina-wiegman-could-manage-in-mens-football

FA, 'Women's and girls' football in numbers, 2017/18 season' infographic, www.thefa.com/-/media/thefacom-new/files/womens/fa_womens_girls_in_numbers_info-graphic_2017-18.ashx

FA, 'Vitality Women's FA Cup season 2022/23 prize fund payments', www.thefa.com/-/media/thefacom-new/files/

competitions/2022-23/womens-fa-cup/vitality-womens-fa-cup-prize-fund.ashx

FA, 'Inspiring positive change: strategy update', November 2022, www.thefa.com/-/media/thefacom-new/files/womens/2022-23/the-fas-inspiring-positive-change-two-year-strategy-update-november-2022.ashx

Feringa, Megan, 'The three trailblazers who walked into an office, left with a national football team and altered the course of Wales Women history', October 7, 2022 www.walesonline.co.uk/sport/football/three-trailblazers-who-walked-office-25189886

Forstmann, Nicolas et al, 'Does maternity during sports career jeopardize future athletic success in elite marathon runners?', *European Journal of Sport Science*, June 26, 2022 www.tandfonline.com/doi/full/10.1080/17461391.2022.2089054?scroll=top&needAccess=true&role=tab

Forsyth, JJ et al, 'Menstrual cycle, hormonal contraception and pregnancy in women's football: perceptions of players, coaches and managers', *Sport in Society*, September 27, 2022

Guardian, 'Theresa finds a gap in the FA's defence', June 9, 1979 www.theguardian.com/theguardian/1979/jun/09/1

Lindblom, Hanna et al, 'Extended Knee Control programme lowers weekly hamstring, knee and ankle injury prevalence compared with an adductor strength programme or self-selected injury prevention exercises in adolescent and adult amateur football players: a two-armed cluster-randomised trial with an additional comparison arm', *British Journal of Sports Medicine*, Vol 57, Issue 2, January 2023 bjsm.bmj.com/content/57/2/83

Lopez, Sue, *Women on the Ball*, 1979, Scarlet Press

McNamee, Kathleen, 'Chelsea's Hayes on men's coaching role: I'm not looking for another job', February 2, 2021 www.espn.co.uk/football/chelsea-women/story/4305067/ chelseas-hayes-on-mens-coaching-role-im-not-looking-for-another-job

Okholm Kryger, Katrine et al, 'Ten questions in sports engineering: technology in elite women's football', *Sports Engineering*, November 16, 2022 www.ncbi.nlm.nih.gov/ pmc/articles/PMC9667860/

Owen, Wendy, *Kicking Against Tradition*, 2005, History Press

Perry, Carly et al, 'Elite female footballers in England: an exploration of mental ill-health and help-seeking intentions', *Science and Medicine in Football*, June 5, 2022

PFA, 'Emma Mukandi calls for improved support for new mothers in the WSL', January 12, 2023 www.thepfa. com/news/2023/1/12/emma-mukandi--improved-support-for-new-mothers

Selman, Rachel et al, 'Maximizing recovery in the postpartum period: a timeline for rehabilitation from pregnancy through return to sport', *International Journal of Sports Physical Therapy*, Vol 17, Issue 6, 2022, ijspt.scholasticahq.com/article/37863.pdf

Sky Sports, 'Sarina Wiegman: England Women boss says she is 'not worried' about Australia ending their 30-game unbeaten run', April 12, 2023 www.skysports.com/football/news/12010/12855423/sarina-wiegman-england-women-boss-says-she-is-not-worried-about-australia-ending-their-30-game-unbeaten-run

Tomas, Fiona, 'Fara Williams interview: Women's football must address its 'fat club' culture', June 10, 2022 www.telegraph.co.uk/football/2022/06/10/fara-williams-interview-womens-football-must-address-fat-club/

Walden, Markus and Hagglund, Martin, 'Knee Control Study Project', utbildning.sisuforlag.se/fotboll/tranare/spelarutbildning/knakontroll-engelska/the-study/

WalesOnline.co.uk, 'UEFA take action... by fining Wales!' May 8, 2003 www.walesonline.co.uk/sport/football/football-news/uefa-take-action-fining-wales-2484003

Williams, Jean, 'Women's football, Europe and professionalization, 1971-2001' uefaacademy.com/wp-content/uploads/sites/2/2019/05/20110622_Williams-Jean_Final-Report.pdf

Wilson, Jeremy, 'Terri Bennett relieves day she took fight to play football with boys all way to High Court – when she was just 12', April 24, 2020 www.telegraph.co.uk/football/2020/04/24/terri-bennett-relieves-day-took-fight-play-football-boys-way/

Wrack, Suzanne, 'Mary Earps angry that fans cannot buy her England shirt', July 20, 2023 https://www.theguardian.com/football/2023/jul/20/mary-earps-angry-england-goalkeeper-shirt-womens-world-cup